A Book About Sweet Peas
History, Culture, Varieties and Uses of Sweet Peas

by Walter P. Wright

with an introduction by Roger Chambers

This work contains material that was originally published in 1909.

This publication was created and published for the public benefit, utilizing public funding and is within the Public Domain.

This edition is reprinted for educational purposes and in accordance with all applicable Federal Laws.

Introduction Copyright 2018 by Roger Chambers

Self Reliance Books

Get more historic titles on animal and stock breeding, gardening and old fashioned skills by visiting us at:

http://selfreliancebooks.blogspot.com/

Introduction

I am pleased to present yet another title on Gardening.

The work is in the Public Domain and is re-printed here in accordance with Federal Laws.

As with all reprinted books of this age that are intended to perfectly reproduce the original edition, considerable pains and effort had to be undertaken to correct fading and sometimes outright damage to existing proofs of this title. At times, this task is quite monumental, requiring an almost total "rebuilding" of some pages from digital proofs of multiple copies. Despite this, imperfections still sometimes exist in the final proof and may detract from the visual appearance of the text.

I hope you enjoy reading this book as much as I enjoyed making it available to readers again.

Roger Chambers

JESSIE CUTHBERTSON.
Rose flake on cream ground. See Appendix.

PRINCE OLAF.
A blue flake. See Appendix

MRS. WILCOX.
Red Flake. A waved or Spencer form of America. See Appendix.

PREFACE.

I HAVE made an earnest attempt in this book to show how much of interest, charm and pleasure lie in the Sweet Pea, while giving ample practical information as to its culture.

We must not limit our thoughts of great garden flowers to a calculation of how many barrow-loads of manure are required to win a certain silver cup with them. We must take into account the joy which their beauty and perfume bring into our lives, and the uplifting impulses which arise out of a conception of the creative forces which lie enfolded within their petals. In doing this we need not forget the spade and manure.

No flower can influence human lives more strongly than the little Sweet Pea. Suitable for culture in the smallest as in the largest of gardens, beautiful alike in form and colour, possessing a delicious odour, it further enchains our interest by the glimpses which Mendelian experiments with it have given us into the half revealed mysteries of the laws which govern the creation of new plants.

I hope that the simple verses with which the chapters are introduced will not so far offend purists in prosody as to neutralise the pleasure that other parts of the book may possibly give them.

WALTER P. WRIGHT.

December, 1909.

CONTENTS.

[For General Index see the end of the volume.]

CHAPTER.	PAGE
I.—OF THE BEAUTY AND PERFUME OF THE SWEET PEA	9
II.—OF THE INTRODUCTION OF THE SWEET PEA, AND ITS RISE INTO PUBLIC FAVOUR	13
III.—OF THE STRUCTURE OF THE SWEET PEA FLOWER, SELF-FERTILISATION, CROSS-FERTILISATION, THE LAWS OF MENDEL, AND OTHER MATTERS CONNECTED WITH RAISING NEW VARIETIES	24
IV.—OF THE SEEDS OF SWEET PEAS AND THE RAISING OF PLANTS, WITH A WORD AS TO CUTTINGS	36
V.—OF THE BEST SOILS AND MANURES FOR SWEET PEAS	47
VI.—OF THE METHODS OF PLANTING AND SUPPORTING SWEET PEAS	52
VII.—OF THE PLACES IN WHICH SWEET PEAS MAY BE GROWN, HOW THEY MAY BE USED IN BEDS AND HERBACEOUS BORDERS, AND ON WALLS AND FENCES	57
VIII.—OF THE SWEET PEA AS AN EXHIBITION FLOWER	64
IX.—OF THE SWEET PEA AS A MARKET FLOWER	70
X.—OF THE SWEET PEA UNDER GLASS	74
XI.—OF THE ENEMIES OF THE SWEET PEA	79
XII.—OF THE VARIETIES OF SWEET PEAS	85
XIII.—OF THE SWEET PEA IN ENGLISH COTTAGE GARDENS	93
XIV.—OF THE SWEET PEA IN SCOTTISH GARDENS	98
XV.—OF THE SWEET PEA IN WALES AND THE WEST COUNTRY	101
XVI.—OF THE SWEET PEA IN IRISH GARDENS	105
XVII.—OF THE SWEET PEA IN THE BRITISH COLONIES	107
XVIII.—OF THE SWEET PEA IN THE UNITED STATES OF AMERICA	111
XIX.—OF WOMAN'S INFLUENCE ON THE SWEET PEA	115
XX.—THE SWEET PEA GROWER'S A.B.C.	119
APPENDIX.—A CATALOGUE OF VARIETIES OF SWEET PEAS WITH SELECTIONS	142
INDEX	165

LIST OF ILLUSTRATIONS.

PORTRAIT OF WALTER P. WRIGHT	*Frontispiece.*	
PRINCESS VICTORIA (DOBBIE)	*Facing p.*	14
SWEET PEA LEAVES EATEN BY A LOOPER CATERPILLAR	,,	15
RAISING SWEET PEAS IN POTS	,,	24
A STURDY, WELL-ROOTED SWEET PEA SEEDLING	,,	25
A WEAK SWEET PEA PLANT	,,	32
AUTUMN SOWN SWEET PEAS	,,	33
NORA UNWIN	,,	40
ETTA DYKE	,,	41
HELEN PIERCE	,,	48
PARADISE IVORY	,,	49
SWEET PEA AND ROSE BEAUTY (Coloured plate)	,,	56
SUNPROOF CRIMSON	,,	64
THE MARQUIS	,,	65
JOHN INGMAN	,,	72
KING EDWARD SPENCER	,,	73
SWEET PEAS AT THE RIGHT STAGE FOR CROSS-FERTILISING OR GATHERING TO PACK	,,	80
A LOOSE SPIKE AND A WELL-FILLED SPIKE	,,	80
STAKING SWEET PEAS	,,	81
SWEET PEA AND ROSE BEAUTY (Coloured plate)	,,	88
SWEET PEAS GROWN IN FRONT OF A GARDEN SHED	,,	96
A TYPICAL POT OF SWEET PEAS	,,	97
CONSTANCE OLIVER	,,	104
ZERO	,,	105
ZARINA	,,	112
AZURE FAIRY	,,	113
A VASE OF SWEET PEAS	,,	120
A BOWL OF SWEET PEAS	,,	121
MRS. CHARLES FOSTER	,,	128
ASTA OHN	,,	129
AUDREY CRIER	,,	136
MRS. WILCOX	,,	137
PRINCE OLAF	,,	144
JESSIE CUTHBERTSON	,,	145

DIAGRAMS IN TEXT.

FIG.		PAGE
1.	SWEET PEAS AND BEES	27
2.	SWEET PEA FLOWER AFTER THE PETALS HAVE GONE	28
3.	SWEET PEA AT THE RIGHT STAGE FOR CROSS FERTILISATION	29
4.	SWEET PEA FLOWER EMASCULATED	29
5.	SEED AND SEEDLING OF SWEET PEA	40
6.	RAISING SWEET PEAS IN POTS	42
7.	PLANTS IN POTS—WHEN TO SUPPORT THEM	54
8.	STAKES AND STRING FOR SUPPORTING CLUMP OF SWEET PEAS	55
9.	SYDENHAM'S WIRE LADDER SUPPORT FOR SWEET PEAS	56
10.	JONES'S EXHIBITION OR TABLE VASE FOR SWEET PEAS	69
11.	GROWING SWEET PEAS IN POTS	76
12.	A SPRAY AT THE RIGHT STAGE TO GATHER FOR PACKING	129

A BOOK ABOUT SWEET PEAS.

CHAPTER I.

OF THE BEAUTY AND PERFUME OF THE SWEET PEA.

> You ask me what I see in tiny you
>   That's better than the others?
> There's just one little sparkling drop of dew
>   That's brighter than its brothers.
>
> You ask me why I leave the friendly throng
>   To be with you alone?
> There's always one dear warbling linnet's song
>   That's purest in its tone.
>
> You ask me why, in hard-snatched leisure hour,
>   'Tis you I'm always seeking?
> Because the perfume of one special flower
>   Is sweetest in its greeting.
>
> You ask me why I keep you by my side?
>   You ask me why I love you?
> Your clinging tendrils take my hand and guide
>   My steps to realms above you.

DO we love Roses, Carnations or Chrysanthemums less, because we love Sweet Peas more? I write beside a Cornish sea. The crests of the waves in the bay of St Ives break white as snow, but the seamews' breasts seem whiter still.

There are flowers as beautiful, as fragrant, as the Sweet Pea, but none so appealing. Is it the grace of the fluttering shapes that dance so lightly above the supporting sticks, or the mute pleading of the slender tendrils which grope for a friendly hand, or the lovely tints that overlie the dainty blossoms? We cannot answer. We know that they win our love and sympathy as well as our admiration.

It is easy to grow Sweet Peas, because they are in our hearts. They spring into radiant life under hands that are softened by affection. The beginner succeeds with them at the outset, for he gives them the gentle touch of instinctive love. No weary period of probation tries him, beauty comes swiftly into being.

There is no flower of the first rank that is so rapidly, so generously responsive as the Sweet Pea. Note the bursting leaves, the extending stems, the eager buds. See how they press each other in the race for beauty. The plant loves to bloom. It experiences a passionate joy in flinging out its glorious largesse of blossom. It pours out flowers as a thrush pours out song It loves the sunny haunts of old gardens, and finds joy in every hour of the summer.

The Sweet Pea is the dearest because it is the most companionable of flowers. Its frank delight in existence arouses a responsive impulse in breasts that are growing cold to the world. Reader, has the time come with you when you have asked yourself whether it is all worth while—the strife, the burden, the pain of a life that was once very fair ? Has the spring-time lost its magic, the sea its glamour, the countryside its message, the fruit its flavour ? If the answer is in the affirmative, my duty is clear; it is to take you by the hand, lead you into my Sweet Pea garden, and teach you its joys. There you will find new hope, new courage, new interest, new youth.

Let me show you the simple but beautiful structure of the Sweet Pea flower. It is made up of four parts. The largest is an upright one at the top of the flower, and is called the standard. Two petals spread right and left just below it: they are called the wings. The fourth part is folded in so as to form a little sac, and it hangs at the bottom of the flower: it is called the keel. Standard, wings, and keel! We succumb at once to the temptation of obvious parallels. On its wings our floral butterfly soars afar, on its keel it seeks distant seas. These figures of fancy are as inevitable as they are harmless.

In simple, unstudied beauty the Sweet Pea has no superior amid all the flowers of the garden. Its tints are exquisite and varied. We get soft pearls and ivories and opals, and the pure whiteness of the Alpine snow. The softened yellow of Cornish cream vies with the primrose of the woodland. The rich yellow of the Buttercup and the Tulip, or even of the Gorse which spreads over the rocky hills around my window, is denied to us as yet, but we are nearer than we used to be, and the time may come when it is given to us. It always seems to me that the approach to yellow is nearer in those flowers which have pink or rose in a belt upon the edge of the petals than in any of the selfs. Shall we reach yellow, then, by a by-road ? No matter, so that we really get it.

These same bordered flowers, with some approach to yellow as to their body, are painted with a wondrous and exquisite delicacy. Sunset lights glow in their warm tints.

The pinks are many, from the soft hue that merely shines through white to the brilliant colour that is as full of character and decision as a zonal Geranium. These are the colours for people who adorn their rooms with flowers, because they are as beautiful by night as they are by day. Rose, cerise, carmine, crimson and scarlet are all represented. A bold florist introduces a magenta now and then, but it is flung forth with scorn.

The pale blue of the sky has never so pearly a tint as when a floating belt of cumulus passes slowly beneath it. This coveted shade we get in Sweet Peas, with many another of blue, from French grey to purple, claret and maroon. But we have not quite touched the glistening, pellucid blue of Salvia patens.

We have many pretty parti-coloured flowers—rose, blue or purple on white, rose standard and peacock wings, and other combinations.

In all there is that delicious perfume which is the soul of the flower. The reproach cannot be levelled at raisers of Sweet Peas, as at raisers of Carnations, that varieties without fragrance have been multiplied. The newest Sweet Pea has all the odour of the oldest. Take what colour we will, the Sweet Pea is the *sweet* Pea still.

But after all, little has been said when only beauty of form, variety of colour and constancy of perfume have been eulogised. There still remains the Sweet Pea as a plant—that lightsome, free-hearted, happy plant which blossoms so early, so abundantly, and so long. Its flowers dance and sparkle in the sunlight the whole summer through, ever changing, yet ever beautiful. We cut armfuls, basketfuls of flowers. We cut day by day. Still the plant smiles on the steel, and pursues its beneficent way.

Is it not a delicious thought that everyone can grow this beautiful flower?

Too old at forty, or even eighty, does not apply to Sweet Pea growers. A man who takes them up at seventy has just learned how to feel his way to the true enjoyment of life, and may look forward with every confidence to a green and happy old age, whatever his past may have been.

As to the other sex, all women love Sweet Peas. And their love is real love—love unqualified, undiluted, untinged by pedantry, or love of controversy, or desire to beat another grower in the show tent. It is the flower for its own sake —the gracious, delicate, winning blossom, with its appealing charm of form, colour and perfume, not for its possibilities as a winner of cups, medals and money.

Is the inference gatherable that all of the sterner sex grow Sweet Peas for cups, medals or cash? I do not mean that. It is far otherwise. But I think it may be said fairly that the average woman's love for Sweet Peas is purer and more disinterested than the average man's. You do not grudge her this credit, my reader? You do not become angry with me, and, hunting out my name as a winner of prizes for Sweet Peas in past years, cry, " Out upon this man as a blatant hypocrite, who prates of pure devotion and himself pockets cash won in competitions?" You understand, do you not, that I am less concerned to condemn competitions than to lay a tribute of respectful homage at the feet of our wives and sisters? Let us vie with each other in offering chivalrous acknowledgment of their unsullied love for our beautiful flower—and try and beat each other just the same.

In truth, there is pleasure in the merry joust. It is inspiring to see lances broken and shields rung. And among those who gather round the lists to see the knights perform there must be many who receive their first impulse to become participators. They see Sweet Peas of rare beauty—the finest products of the best cultivators, and they are ravished, enchanted. They gaze in wonder. They eagerly fill notebooks with names. They buttonhole growers, and hurl forth a heavy bombardment of questions about soils and seeds, manures and varieties. They stuff pockets with pamphlets and catalogues, which are perused with thirsty eagerness on the way home, and after the evening meal. They have seen something which has been a great revelation to them. New horizons have opened out before them. They have found that rarest of treasures after the rubicon of forty has been passed—a new interest in life. What system of philosophy, what raking of libraries, what expenditure on travel, what zeal in the collection of works of art, could do more for them than the beauty and perfume of this little flower?

Rally, my brothers! rally, my sisters! to this gentle and flowing standard. Rejoice when you think that in a few short weeks it may be floating over your own garden.

Gather, my brothers! gather, my sisters! under these perfumed and protecting wings. And let your hearts swell at the thought that as long as life is with you they may remain your shield from depression and despair.

Go forth, my brothers! go forth, my sisters! on this trusty keel, which the winds of adversity cannot overwhelm, nor the waves of worldly trouble drown.

CHAPTER II.

OF THE INTRODUCTION OF THE SWEET PEA, AND ITS RISE INTO PUBLIC FAVOUR.

When history's re-written I hope you will pardon
A version that's born in the peace of a garden;
It touches a matter of national weight,
No less than the union that made Britain great;
For the will that made England and Scotland one Power
First sprang in men's hearts through the love of a flower,
The stroke of the sword had failed as a plea
And victory was won by the little Sweet Pea.

It came from the South in the days of Queen Anne
(The news that she's dead you regretfully scan),
And Southron and Scot, still half longing to fight,
Were charmed with the flower, and made haste to unite.
They saw that with enemies over the seas
They had better, themselves, battle mainly with Peas;
So they hastened to smother their ancient dislikes—
To bring out the spades and to store all the pikes.

And ever since then the cool Sassenach's lot
Has been to keep peace with the fire-headed Scot.
The task has been easy, as fights with the Rose
Form an adequate vent for the oldest of foes.
The exhibitor's tube takes the place of a gun,
And, between you and me, it's far healthier fun.
The Carnation, the Pansy, the Aster, the Stock,
Keep hands from sharp blades, and hot heads from the block.

THE Sweet Pea came to us from the South—from sunny Italy. There are some flower-lovers who want to hear every scrap of information which somebody else can collect for them about their favourite, and so I am going to tell how and when the Sweet Pea came. Practical folk may skip all this, of course. They want to know how to manure ground, when to sow seed, and so forth; and they do not care in the least where the Sweet Pea came from, or indeed, if it never came from anywhere at all, but just " growed." These good folk will begin their innings in Chapter IV., to which, if they take no interest in derivation and development, I respectfully refer them.

SWEET PEA LEAVES EATEN BY A LOOPER CATERPILLAR.
See Chapter XI.

had not quite so many names as his famous Pear, which rejoices in an odd score of synonyms, but he was variously referred to as Uvedale, Udale, and Udal. Miller refers to him in his *Gardener's Dictionary*, first published in 1731, as " Dr. Udal, of Enfield, a curious collector and introducer of many rare exoticks, plants and flowers."

It is a little distressing to find that we were behind the Dutch, however. Their botanists must have got seeds from Cupani before Dr. Uvedale, or how is it that they were able to illustrate the plant in the *Horti-Medeci Amstelodamensis* between 1697 and 1701 ? Commelin, the Dutch botanist who provided the material for this engraving, or some other person acting as editor, decided to leave nothing to chance in naming the plant. He enveloped it in the all-embracing, comprehensive, if somewhat staggering term of *Lathyrus distoplatyphyllus hirsutis mollis et odorus*. The prudent amateur tactician will not attempt to take a fortress of this kind by storm. He will sit down before it, and reduce it by sap and mine.

The whole of it was cut down to *odoratus* eventually by Linnæus (1707-1778), who was a child when the plant was first distributed in northern Europe.

The value of a species lies more in its capacity for producing varietal forms than in its own intrinsic beauty, however great that may be. Directly a plant begins to show variations, keen horticultural noses begin to sniff. There is no knowing what it may lead to. Human nature being what it is, an amateur no sooner gets a pretty red plant than he wants a white form of it ; no sooner a white than a yellow ; no sooner a yellow than a blue, and so on.

The Sweet Pea proved to be a most interesting, exciting and tantalising species, in that it went just far enough to prove that it could produce varieties if it liked, and then desisted.

The first Sweet Pea had purple flowers, and a list published 100 years afterwards could only muster four, which were respectively (or were called respectively) black, scarlet, white, and variegated (Painted Lady). What disgust the floriculturists must have felt at this slow progress!

A good many would turn from it in despair, and certainly the Sweet Pea attracted so little attention that it is doubtful if any records could be found giving the exact date of the introduction of the famous Black, Scarlet, White and Painted Lady. We know that John Mason, of the Orange Tree, in Fleet Street, London, offered them in 1793, and there we stop. We hope that the Orange Tree was a fact, but we fear that it was only a sign, like the Red Lion swinging above an inn. But we like to think of something distinctly horticultural in Fleet Street, anyway, if it was only painted on a board, because the modern associations of that delectable thoroughfare are so entirely devoid of garden charm. Probably the site of the Orange Tree is now a newspaper office, and over the sacred threshold where gaitered squires up by coach from the country walked to buy seeds of Master John Mason, hurry young reporters, eager to interview the latest murderess, tell us exactly what she likes for dinner, get her portrait from childhood up, and generally interest, educate and amuse the rising generation.

We should have liked to see the Sweet Peas which John Mason sold to the gaitered squires (let us call a typical one Beeves Urmsing, senior, regarding him as an ancestor of George Meredith's Beeves Urmsing), over the counter at the sign of the Orange Tree—nay, we should have liked to trot behind the portly Beeves, with his huge hat, high stock and resounding top-boots from the very moment that he alighted from the coach in the Borough High Street, and made his way to Fleet Street. Charged with strict injunctions from Dame Urmsing, and religiously striving to remember them in spite of the distractions caused by the scenes around him, and by anticipations of the coming night's outing with an old Cambridge friend (well-known to have developed a fine discrimination in port) Beeves stalks along.

John Mason's shop is full of the smells of seeds and herbs. A stack of drawers rises to the ceiling, which, to be sure, is not very high. These drawers are marked with mysterious abbreviations, like those of a chemist. White canvas bags, with the tops folded back to show a wide open mouth, contain the more common seeds.

John Mason, apprised of the quality of his customer, appears in person from a dim recess screened by a green curtain, with his quill along his ear, and his wig hastily adjusted to a new and extraordinary angle. Yes, he has the famous Black, Scarlet, White and Painted Lady Sweet Peas. He relieves the overcharged Beeves of his message. He will certainly send the famous Sweet Peas, together with all the other floral treasures which the Dame wants. He hopes the Squire will kindly permit him to mention his (Beeves Urmsing's) name when posting catalogues to the nobility and gentry in his neighbourhood. He begs respectfully to suggest that careful watch be kept against slugs when the famous Sweet Peas come through the ground. He can supply a magnificent strain of ten-week Stocks, certain to produce a large proportion of double flowers, and he laughs heartily (although not so uproariously as Beeves himself) when the Squire drags in a joke about neck stocks, and whether the wearers thereof see single or double after their third bottle.

We should have liked to see all this, and we should have liked to see the flowers themselves later on, when they had opened in Dame Urmsing's garden. I am afraid that the famous Black had very little more beauty in it than the swarthy opponent of Tom Cribb, whose illustrious name I take shame in acknowledging that I forget. It would probably be a dirty purple or maroon. Then as to the Scarlet, had not a little imagination been brought into play concerning it? Was it really scarlet? I think that the first variety of that colour was Scarlet Gem, and that did not appear until many years after the axe had been laid to the root of the Orange Tree, and the fell scythesman had cut down worthy John Mason. Whatever it was, Dame Urmsing probably found it very useful for placing on her dinner table. The White was all right, of course: it was genuine. As for the Painted Lady, it was a comparatively old variety in 1793. The Catalogue of the National Sweet Pea Society tells us that it was one of the earliest of the varieties of *Lathyrus odoratus*. The standard was rose-coloured, and the wings were white, or white with a blush suffusion.

Only this quartette after nearly a hundred years! What were our florists doing? In the light of present-day knowledge we are compelled to think that they were not very wideawake. They were dealing with other things, of course, and had but half an eye to spare for the Sweet Pea. They were engaged with Roses, Carnations, Auriculas, Verbenas, Pelargoniums, Tulips, and other favourites of their day. Being so engrossed, they missed the secret that Nature had cunningly hidden away in the Sweet Pea, as it had hidden radium and aviation, for a later generation to discover.

First, how did the Black, the Scarlet, the White and the Painted Lady, offered by John Mason at the sign of the Orange Tree, come into being? The Pea which Cupani sent to Dr. Uvedale was purple, and perhaps the Black was a selection from it a little darker in colour. But the Scarlet? Even supposing that the florist who first described it as scarlet was slightly affected with that distressing malady colour blindness, which affects so many of the same profession at the present day, and that it was not really a scarlet, still, we must concede that it was a considerable remove from purple. Perhaps it was rose, or carmine, or magenta. Whatever it was the question remains to be answered: How was it got? The budding horticulturist replies glibly, "By sporting." To the further question: What is a sport? he answers, "A natural variation thrown by a plant without any cross fertilisation."

Admittedly many plants do throw variations without any apparent influence of pollination from another flower. The Chrysanthemum is a familiar example. You grow a collection of Chrysanthemums, and one branch of a particular plant bears a flower different from the blooms on the other shoots. The grower eagerly propagates from that branch, and gets a stock of plants which bear flowers similar to the new-comer —the "sport." He can sell the novelty at once, and it will keep its character, probably, for a long time, and may or may not sport in turn in some future year. Fortunes have been made with flower "sports," and consequently the trade florist looks upon them with complacent eye. But can we say that the Sweet Pea is a sportive plant? Recollect that century which elapsed before John Mason of the Orange Tree (now I think of it, was the Orange Tree flourishing at the time that Samuel Johnson was living in Gough Square?) was able to offer the famous Four. One can hardly call a species sportive when it progresses at that tortoise-like rate. Really, I doubt whether any one of the Four was a sport. As I have said already, the acquisition of the Black by means of selection from the purple is a safe assumption, because the colour of the species would vary naturally, to some extent, with differences of soil. I think that the famous Scarlet and the famous White must have come from natural cross-fertilisation. Yes, I know all about the structure of the flower. I know the secret that the Sweet Pea guarded so long, but which we have discovered at last. I am well aware that it adopted in its youth an ingenious device for avoiding natural cross-fertilisation, no less a plan, indeed, than ripening its pollen and getting self-fertilised while still in the bud.

(This was an extraordinary proceeding on the part of the plant. In elaborate treatises Darwin has shown us the marvellous structure of many flowers—a structure that seems impossible of explanation on any other ground than that the flowers were bent on securing cross-fertilisation. But in the Sweet Pea we have an example to the contrary. It obviously does not want cross-fertilisation, else why should it adopt a plan and structure that throw almost insuperable obstacles in the way of cross-fertilisation?)

I repeat that I am familiar with the fact that the Sweet Pea is ripe for fertilisation while the flower remains closed tightly, and thus guards against bees bringing pollen from other flowers, or the wind from scattering it. But still I think that cross-fertilisation must have been at work. As long as I have known Sweet Peas I have been acquainted with a tiny dark beetle—a slow-moving, sedate, gentle little creature—which crawls about inside the flowers. I do not think that this beetle leads to cross-fertilisation generally by conveying pollen from bloom to bloom, because I think that in the vast majority of cases the flower was self-fertilised before the beetle gained access to it; but I think that every now and then something happened—a bud was torn perhaps —and so foreign pollen got in, either through the medium of wind, beetle, or bee. With this crossing the colour fixity was disturbed and a new hue came.

If I arrive at this conclusion by a process of attrition— by the elimination of all other means of explanation—I hold it none the less firmly. It is not impossible, to say the least of it. It explains everything that cannot be explained otherwise.

There is an extremely interesting stage in the history of the development of the Sweet Pea, and that concerns a variety named Blue Edged, which was distributed by the well-known seedsman, James Carter, of High Holborn, London, in 1860. Carter purchased the Pea from Major Trevor Clarke, who had reputedly produced it by crossing a white Sweet Pea with another species of Lathyrus called *Magellanicus*. The flower was white with a blue edge. The interest of this Blue Hybrid (it would be correct to describe it as a hybrid if it came from two different species) lies in the fact that artificial cross-fertilisation had been resorted to, and it is remarkable that this operation was not followed up by others immediately. Perhaps it was, but none the less, new varieties still came slowly. Scarlet Invincible, a variety which became very popular and remained a favourite for a long time, did not appear until 1866. It was nearer carmine than scarlet. Two years later a pink German variety called Crown Princess of Prussia appeared, and five years afterwards another German sort with white flowers, called Fairy Queen. Butterfly, white with blue edge, was distributed by Sutton and Sons in 1878, and Invincible Black, Invincible Striped and Violet Queen by James Carter and Co. in 1880.

Progress, it will be seen, had been hastened a little, but it was still slow, and the florists had not yet awakened to the possibilities of the flower. Either they did not know how to cross it, or they did not think it worth crossing. There is a third alternative, and a creditable one—that they raised a good many varieties by cross-fertilisation, but did not distribute them because they could not be "fixed," *i.e.*, kept true to colour. We know how difficult it is to keep some modern Sweet Peas true, and alas! we know how hard raisers, who are in a hurry to get rich, find it to hold a new variety long enough to be sure of its being fixed, when eager amateurs are willing to buy and take risks. The amateur tempts, the raiser yields, and so a variety is distributed while still in a highly nervous and variable state.

Presently the man came who was strong on each of the three salient points: (1) he knew how to cross Sweet Peas; (2) he thought that they were worth crossing; (3) he was not in a hurry to get rich; and consequently he would not sell a novelty until he was quite sure that it would keep true. Let us doff our hats to Henry Eckford, not in noisy applause, for he has gone to join John Mason in the Happy Garden Grounds, but in respectful silence.

It was Henry Eckford who made the Sweet Pea the great flower that it is. It was he who gave it its huge public. He delighted amateurs with new and beautiful colours and with improved form. He enlarged the flower, and added grace, substance and symmetry to it. It was loose—he gave it regularity. It was flimsy—he made it solid. It was ragged—he knit it together. The standard was badly notched —he went a great way to filling the gap up. But mark you, he did all this without robbing the flower of its fragrance. If he had done that—but why speculate? he did not: he kept it as sweet as he found it.

Eckford did so much that there really seemed little more to do when he drew towards the close of his busy and beneficent life. (May I, digressing for a few moments, tell you how he spent those last few years? It was a simple ending. He walked among his Sweet Pea acres, with toddling grandchildren about him, hobnobbed affectionately with such old florist friends as went to see him, talked about the dear companions of his youth, and on his deathbed smiled serenely on the world that he was leaving without fear and without regret. He only shed tears on one occasion, and that was when a band of friends and admirers presented him with a token of esteem and love. So may your life and mine pass, oh my brother, leaving a memory of brightness and perfume behind us when we cross the threshold of the Greater Garden.)

INTRODUCTION OF THE SWEET PEA.

But the Sweet Pea was ever a secretive flower, and at long last, when the secret of her loves, so long held inviolable, had been wrested from her, when all about her seemed known, and when a hundred beautiful daughters surrounded her—then she laid down another card.

As I have said, Eckford had gone a long way to get the disfiguring notch out of the standard. He left it flat, smooth and even. We were not dissatisfied, so far as form was concerned. We had a great deal more than we had ever expected to get, and our only thought of future development was in respect to colour. We had not a Buttercup yellow, we had not a Gentian blue. Give us these, and our cup of bliss would be full. We got a little nearer to both. The stages were slow, but we had grown used to the exercise of patience with Sweet Peas, and we could afford to wait. Time was on our side, the Buttercup yellow and the Gentian blue would surely come.

Something came with a vengeance, but it was not the Buttercup yellow, nor yet the Gentian blue. It was not a development of colour at all, but of form. We gasped in sheer amazement. This astonishing flower had made an absolutely new, revolutionary, cataclysmic, prestidigitatory, thaumaturgic change in the form of its standard. Left comfortably smooth and flat by Eckford, it suddenly threw a variety with a standard that was heavily waved or crinkled.

A waved standard! And with it increased size of flower, greater substance! A crinkled standard in itself might not have vanquished us, for it might have meant a flower of shrivelled and meagre appearance; but Nature seemed to have resolved to carry her new Sweet Pea scheme through thoroughly, and increased the material in the petal to allow for the folds.

The waved flower reigns. While my pen flows along the paper in shaping these words, the thought crosses my mind: Has the Sweet Pea other revolutionary secrets in her keeping? Shall I have to modify the first sentence of this paragraph when I write an introduction to the twenty-fifth edition of the present work? I know not. All I know is that in this, the tenth year of the twentieth century, the waved Sweet Pea reigns.

It reigns supreme, unchallenged. It has taken the Sweet Pea world by storm, and by the appeal of its wonderful beauty has brought thousands of new devotees into the fold. All the world yields to its beauty and grace.

Did Nature manage it unassisted? This is a question of

intense interest. When plants throw sports it is a well-known fact that they generally do so in more than one place simultaneously. The waved Sweet Pea appeared in very fine form in the gardens of Althorp Park, Northampton, and in inferior form in the grounds of a market gardener at Histon, near Cambridge, about the same time. The head gardener at Althorp, Silas Cole, named the former Countess Spencer; the market grower, W. J. Unwin, called the Histon variety Gladys Unwin. Countess Spencer was large, much waved, and rich pink in colour with a deeper edge. Gladys Unwin was smaller, less waved, looser in the wings, and pale pink in hue. As a flower Countess Spencer, when in its best character, was superior to Gladys Unwin; but the latter had an enormous advantage—it was true, whereas Countess Spencer was variable. But there was a third form, and this identical with Countess Spencer. It appeared at Eckford's grounds at Wem. As it was identical he did not give it a name of his own, but sold it as Countess Spencer.

Now we come to the vital question: Whence came these flowers? Here are the reports of the various growers:—

Countess Spencer (Silas Cole): Raised by crossing Prima Donna with a seedling in 1899. The seedling itself was the result of a cross between the well-known varieties Triumph and Lovely, and was unfixed.

Gladys Unwin (W. J. Unwin): Appeared in a row of Prima Donna. There was no artificial crossing.

Eckford waved (Eckford): Appeared among Prima Donna without artificial crossing.

We are still left groping, but one fact stands out, namely, that Countess Spencer certainly emanated from Prima Donna. The latter was a pink variety, with a plain standard, and it did what few of the old varieties did—bore four flowers on each stem—a character which is one of the strongest features of the waved Sweet Peas.

Let us go back to the Althorp Park waved pink. Its three parents (if we may count Triumph and Lovely as parents) were all plain standards. It was not true. Two of the earliest variations which appeared in it were (1) Carmine standard and rose wings—named John Ingman; (2) Orange—called Hon. Mrs. C. R. Spencer. (The latter name dropped out, as the same variation appeared elsewhere, and being exhibited first under the name of Helen Lewis, Hon. Mrs. C. R. Spencer was merged in the latter.)

Is the reader unable to understand why the waved pink should be true at Wem and Histon, and unfixed at Althorp?

He is given the following explanation: The stock of seed was disposed of to a florist, and a few pods of seed from another cross (Countess Spencer ✕ Salopian) were mixed in by accident. The seed was sent to California to be grown, as it was thought that with the dry climate there a good harvest could be better relied on than in Great Britain. The admixture of the other cross led to various colours appearing in what should have been a pure pink.

We cannot quite get to the bottom of the derivation of the waved Sweet Pea, but this we know—that we have it. You, dear reader, who grow Sweet Peas merely for adding to the beauty of your garden, and for adorning your rooms, will tell me that the main fact is enough for you. But you have a friend who is a most terrible fellow for probing things, and who can never rest until he has got to the root of every mystery. He will want to inquire farther, and I do not discourage him, although I believe that his quest will prove baffling.

Both of you will find interest and pleasure in Sweet Peas. Both of you will cordially subscribe to my statement that the Sweet Pea stands in the front rank of garden flowers. Both of you will murmur a respectful "Hear, Hear" when I say that we owe a debt of gratitude to the old-time florists who, with loving and patient care, developed this garden treasure, and handed it, a bright and sparkling gem, into our keeping. Both of you will support me when I say that we have made a firm and unswerving resolve to pass it on, when our day ends, not less pure, not less beautiful, not less fragrant than we received it. Thus, and thus only, shall we have exercised a worthy stewardship.

CHAPTER III.

OF THE STRUCTURE OF THE SWEET PEA FLOWER, SELF-FERTILISATION, CROSS-FERTILISATION, THE LAWS OF MENDEL, AND OTHER MATTERS CONNECTED WITH RAISING NEW VARIETIES.

> Mankind, when it first learned to dig,
>   Never suffered sartorial woes,
> The glossy green leaves of the Fig
>   Met all its requirements in clothes.
> Simplicity, bland and benign,
>   Prevailed in both clothing and food,
> And woad was the visible sign
>   Of the warrior's cantankerous mood.
>
> When the Sweet Pea reached Albion's shore
>   Its standard was modest and plain,
> Nor waving nor frilling it bore,
>   And it suffered no harm from the rain.
> To-day in its Spencerised pride,
>   It sniffs at that plain-standard weed,
> Its furbelows spread far and wide,
>   But there's a very poor harvest of seed!

FLOWER of my heart, do you charge me with inconstancy when you see that I begin to speak of ways of changing you? Am I not satisfied with you as you are that I do this thing? Ah! bear with poor mutable humanity, ever driven on by the desire for change. We who enthrone you in our gardens as the reigning queen pay you homage gladly, and would strike down anyone who dared to disparage you. Our love, our admiration, our respect, our loyalty, are beyond all question.

Why are we not content to leave you as you are? Were ever subjects satisfied with the extent of their monarch's dominion, with the richness of her person, with the beauty of the jewels in her crown? Did they not ever strive to give her wider territories, a more magnificent court, a richer splendour? Their pride in her is so great, their anxiety that she should make an overwhelming impression upon others, is so intense, that they are ever seeking to add to her beauty.

It is hard to cease when a labour of love has been carried far on towards fruition, and so we still go on. The Sweet Pea has beauty of form—we strive to add still more grace. It has great variety of colour—we endeavour to get fresh hues.

We learned the sex secret of the Sweet Pea in our second chapter. We saw that it differed from many flowers in making provisions against cross-fertilisation, not only by enveloping its vital organs in a close sac, but, recognising that this might not be enough, by providing that the stigma should be viscid and the pollen ripe while the flower was still unexpanded. Let us put this matter to the test. We pick off a flower stem carrying, say, three blooms in various stages of development. One flower is open, another is half expanded, the third is a bud. We see nothing but the floral segments in any of them—no sign of the organs of sex. The expanded flower carries its standard upright or a little "hooded," its wings well spread, its keel closed and upturned like the beak of a bird. (By the way, is it the standard or the keel that is composed of two petals which have amalgamated? That careful student of Sweet Peas, Mr. Charles H. Curtis, says the former; but two botanical works on my shelves say the latter.) Now we make an experiment. With finger and thumb pressed ever so lightly left and right at the base of the keel something happens. A slender yellow stem with a slightly flattened head suddenly darts out, as though propelled by an inner spring, and below it we see a little forest of waving green threads surmounted by reddish heads. The slender stem is the pistil with the stigma or female organ at the top, the green threads are stamens, and the reddish heads are the anthers, which carry the pollen or fertilising powder. The yellow dust that we see is composed of the grains of pollen. Relax the pressure, and the slender stem and threads disappear with the same dramatic swiftness that they sprang out.

Many students who see this go no further. They have studied their Darwin, and become primed with the evidence as to the provision for natural cross-fertilisation. A bee, they will say, alights on the flower, and brings the same pressure to bear on the base of the keel that their fingers and thumb had brought. The parrot beak opens, the organs of sex are exposed, the stigma receives the pollen brought by the bee from a flower previously visited, and the anthers transfer pollen to the body of the bee, to be carried to another bloom; thus natural cross-fertilisation is effected.

Not so fast, friend. Think of the very slow increase in the number of varieties of Sweet Peas—how the flower stood practically still for 150 years—and ask how this can be reconciled with a regular course of natural cross-fertilisation. Bees are older than Sweet Peas. Millions of bees have visited millions of Sweet Pea flowers since Cupani first sent seeds of the lovely annual to Dr. Uvedale of Enfield in 1699, but natural crossing has not resulted. This fact gives you pause, and you carry your investigations a little further. You turn to the partially expanded flower, and you find that the pollen is ripe there also. Interested, you open the keel of the bud, and lo! the pollen in that may be likewise loose. Do bees open Sweet Pea buds? Rarely, if ever. They sometimes pierce the flowers, and an acute observer, Mr. T. H. Dipnall, has drawn my attention to the singular way in which they attack the flower. The bee (a yellow and white banded species) does not alight on the flower itself, but on the calyx. It approaches from one side, and walks round till its body is underneath and its head comes round to the part marked **X** in Fig. 1. Then, if the calyx is intact, it makes a hole. The bee always approaches from the same side and makes the hole in the same place. It might be the same bee and the same flower every time the attack is made. What is the bee in search of? Let us take a flower and draw back the wings. We see that the keel, which is apparently a closed sac, is divided along the curve of the fused carpels (the future pod). We discover also a small horseshoe-shaped opening at the base of the wings (Fig. 1) and a gap made by a curve in the base of the keel. Now the bee makes its hole in the calyx opposite this opening, and by passing its proboscis through, gets access to the nectar at the base of the pod. There is a similar opening on both sides of the flower, and the question arises as to why the bee always chooses one side in preference to the other, as it does.

It is important to observe that this action of bees cannot generally influence cross-fertilisation, because they rarely, if at all, visit buds, and self-fertilisation has taken place before they intervene. Moreover, it is doubtful if they come into contact with the pollen as a rule, because it is borne on anthers high above the base of the keel, and all that they could be likely to touch was surplus pollen that had fallen backwards after self-fertilisation had taken place.

It is possible that the bees affect seeding, as damp may gain access to the base of the pod through the hole they have made. This is not proven. Meanwhile we may well pay a tribute to the acuteness of the bee in discovering exactly the right part of the calyx to attack to find the gap.

Do small beetles get into Sweet Pea buds? Possibly at times, but it is not general. What, then, of natural cross-fertilisation? Simply that it does not, cannot, generally take place. The pistil came up through the cluster of stamens while the bud remained closed, the stigma received pollen, and became self-fertilised. What happens afterwards

Fig. 1.—SWEET PEAS AND BEES.

Left hand.—Wings drawn away from the calyx to show the horse-shoe shaped openings at the base.

Right hand.—The upper figure shows a Sweet Pea flower at the stage when the calyx is perforated (see X); the lower, the flower after the petals have fallen.

has no influence. There may be unlimited pollen-transference at a later stage, but it has no effect. If sufficient pollen grains to fertilise each of the ovules in the ovary (one grain, one ovule) have reached the stigma from the anthers of its own flower, no quantity of pollen grains received by transmission from another flower can have any influence whatever. It explains the very slow development of the Sweet Pea. But

That is the general position—that and no other.
let me hasten to admit the possibility of an odd flower now

and then in the even passage of the years being abnormal, or being injured in the bud, so that an isolated example of natural cross-fertilisation (it seems odd, too, to call it natural if it is accidental) may have taken place. Still more freely let me admit the modification which has been brought about by the advent of the waved standard varieties. In many of these the keel is not closed tightly; still more important, the anthers may be sterile, so that there is no pollen available for the rising stigma, which consequently may be still ripe for fertilisation when the flower opens. Even when the flower has expanded the keel is still nominally closed and the stigma covered, as we have seen already, and consequently cross-fertilisation is not to be expected; but it is certain that the condition presents greater opportunities for it than when the anthers are normally fertile, and the pollen ripe in the bud stage, because pollen often lingers about an expanded flower, and may be blown about by the wind.

Fig. 2.—SWEET PEA FLOWER AFTER THE PETALS HAVE GONE.
Showing the pod, stamens, and pistil. The dotted line represents the keel. Sometimes the stigma protrudes from the keel while the flower is young as here shown.

Some growers have seen the stigma protruding from the keel (Fig 2), and have concluded that such a flower must be liable to cross-fertilisation in any case. What I have said will show them that this is not necessarily so. The question turns upon whether the anthers below are fertile or sterile. If the former, self-fertilisation has taken place before the stigma protruded. With respect to the possibility of cross-fertilisation by the tiny, winged, black beetle (*Meligethes*) which is often found crawling in Sweet Pea flowers, the question turns on whether it can pass from keel to keel while the flower is closed or only half expanded. I think that this is open to grave doubt. I have found the beetle in the keel of expanded flowers, but never in the keel of a bud. If the beetle cannot enter the keel of the undeveloped flower—that is, the flower in its fertilising stage—it cannot, as a general thing, cause cross-fertilisation, although it may do so in exceptional circumstances. Indeed, the same objection that applies to the bee applies to the beetle. The beetle is not new. It existed during the years when Sweet Peas were consistently self-fertilised; why, then, did it have no influence? Let me add, however, that if I were a raiser, to be quite on the safe side I would not, in cross-fertilising, use flowers within whose keel I found the Meligethes.

It is worth while to mention that the leaf-cutter bee (*Megachile*) is credited by some scientists with a power which they deny (erroneously) to the honey-bee—namely, that of depressing the keel of the Sweet Pea and gathering pollen. But it does not open buds, and does not, therefore, cause cross-fertilisation in the natural course of things, because self-fertilisation had taken place before it visited the flower.

Raisers must keep the fact that self-fertilisation is natural constantly before them. Let them examine flowers carefully in every stage, from earliest bud-formation to complete expansion. They will find that the position and state of the stigma change. It develops with the petals. Just before the pollen is ripe the stigma is below the anthers, and is dry. A day or two later it has risen, is among the anthers, is viscid, and is covered with adhering pollen grains. A day

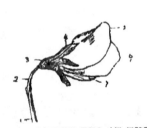

Fig 3.—SWEET PEA AT THE RIGHT STAGE FOR CROSS-FERTILISATION.

1, Stem; 2, Flower-stem; 3, Calyx; 4, Sepals; 5, Standard; 6, Wings; 7, Keel (enclosing organs).

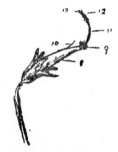

Fig. 4.—SWEET PEA FLOWER EMASCULATED.

8, Fused Carpels (pod); 9, Stamens; 10, Stamen attached to Carpel; 11, Pistil; 12, Style; 13, Stigma.

or two later it is quite above the anthers. Fertilisation (self) will now have taken place, and the formation of the seed pod begun. Mark, all this has happened before the flower is fully open. The keel is still closed, and the stigma covered. The stigma appears outside the keel later on, but it is owing to the rapid development of the seed pod below, and presently the latter also becomes exposed, the petals withering away.

All this emphasises the importance of early action if artificial cross-fertilisation is to be resorted to. The laggard finds himself anticipated by nature. Let him proceed as follows: *First stage*: emasculate the flower while in the bud (Figs. 3 and 4), but leave the keel, and snip off the cohering stamens within it below the anthers with a pair of sharp pointed scissors or small forceps before the pollen sacs have burst. He will generally find it advantageous to operate before any of the flowers on the stem have opened, because if one only has expanded, the buds below are likely to be too forward. He must now wait for the stigma to become viscid, and for pollen to ripen in the flower which he wishes to use as the male parent. The stigma should be covered with the keel, and to guard against foreign pollen anticipating him he may cover the emasculated bud with a bag of waxed paper.

Second stage: Directly the pollen is ready (which may be in two or three days) apply some grains of it to the stigma, and if they adhere all is well, but a little fresh pollen may be applied the following day as a precaution. The keel and bag may be replaced, and the latter left on for a week. The remaining buds on the stem may be picked off. The pollen tubes will pass down to the ovary and fertilise the ovules, which will swell and become seeds. At the same time the united carpels which surround the ovules will begin to develop into a pod.

I have admitted the greater likelihood of natural cross-fertilisation in the modern waved-standards than in the old plain-standards. It is not general, but the chances against it are less numerous than in the case of the plains. Certainly self-fertilisation is much less regular and abundant in the waved than in the plain-standard Sweet Peas. That this is so is certain from the fact that they produce many times less pods per number of flowers. For this reason the seed of waved standards must be always expected to be more expensive than that of plain standards. In the most favourable circumstances the crop of seed is comparatively light, and when the weather is unfavourable it falls almost to nothing. The stamens are less closely in touch with the stigma than in the plain-standard varieties, and often do not touch the tip, which is the sensitive part, at all. The result is that the flower remains unfertilised; when it falls the ovary does not swell, and there is no seed.

There is one comforting reflection for the prospective raiser of new Sweet Peas who has the true facts of fertilisation before him, and that is that the precautions which Nature takes to guard against natural cross-fertilisation make his task much more simple than it is in the case of flowers which court the assistance of wind and bee.

The process of artificial cross-fertilisation is simple and easy—almost too simple, almost too easy, for all and sundry can rush in and cross-fertilise Sweet Peas with as much facility as they can blow their noses. The blowing of a nose may be momentarily irritating to a Sweet Pea amateur who happens to be by if it is noisy, but it has no unpleasant after-effects on him. When, however, the Sweet Pea amateur is bombarded with offers of novelties from all quarters, most of which prove to be unfixed, or identical with others which he has bought at half the price, he is apt to grow " short."

Now that all the world has learned the art of cross-fertilising Sweet Peas, and that the flower has risen to the position of a public favourite, every succeeding year will see a greater influx of reputedly new varieties. What can be done to prevent the country from being flooded with sorts that are only dissimilar in name from existing varieties? Two things, and I earnestly beg every raiser of Sweet Peas to practise them. In the first place, let him grow his novelty for at least three years before he makes any attempt to dispose of it. While he has it in his own garden let him " rogue " it rigorously. (To " rogue " a crop is to pull out every plant which does not conform to the type.) Let him simultaneously take every opportunity of making himself acquainted with all the existing varieties of Sweet Peas. This is not an irksome duty, it is a delightful one. It takes him to Sweet Pea shows, and to the grounds of the growers. When he gets to the shows and the grounds he is with the Sweet Pea Brotherhood. Then he is the happy participator in a gracious companionship, where kindness, good feeling and geniality reign. Those with whom he foregathers are not concerned with the importance of their own social position, nor disposed to inquire as to his. Are they, and he, good florists? Then their credentials are perfect. No more is wanted.

The raiser's second step is to make himself a member of the special society which exists for developing the Sweet Pea, because one of the duties which this excellent body sets itself is the examination and trial of novelties.

We have cross-fertilised our flower, and we see presently that the ovary is swelling and that a pod has formed. We must tie a label on the stem near it, marked with any secret sign which we think fit to adopt, in order to distinguish the cross. And then we wait for the ripening. I advise raisers to make their crosses early in the season, because then there is abundance of time for getting the seed ripe. If flowers are fertilised late in the year—say in August—a long spell of wet weather may retard the ripening; and there seems to be some ground for supposing that slow-ripened seed is uncertain in its germination.

Can new varieties of Sweet Peas be raised by crossing with another species of Lathyrus, or with a variety of such species?

Here is a question of great interest. I have already referred to the statement that Major Trevor Clarke's Blue Hybrid, distributed by James Carter in 1860, was the result of a cross between a variety of *Lathyrus odoratus* and *Lathyrus magellanicus*. The latter is a blue-flowered perennial species, and bears the popular name of Lord Anson's Pea. It must not be confused with the dwarf blue *Lathyrus sativus azureus*, a variety of the Chickling Vetch, which is sold as Lord Anson's Pea not infrequently, but has no right whatever to the name. *L. sativus* came from Southern Europe in 1640, nearly fifty years before Lord Anson was born. *L. magellanicus* is said to have been sent from Cape Horn in 1744, and by a curious coincidence that was the year in which Lord Anson received his promotion as Admiral of the Blue. It would be interesting to try Lord Anson's Pea as a parent again.

With the same regularity as the Sweet Pea grower receives his income-tax papers, he hears of crosses between a variety of Sweet Pea, and the Everlasting Pea, *Lathyrus latifolius*. The latter is a very familiar plant, and is scentless. It is a hardy perennial. The rumours run on much the same lines. The cross has been made—it has taken—the pod has swollen—the seed has been gathered. Interest is excited to a terrific pitch. We have great difficulty in getting to sleep o' nights. But time passes, and we hear no more.

In view of the trouble and confusion which have arisen through the hasty and indiscriminate crossing of Sweet Peas, and of the value of really distinct and reliable novelties, there will be a greater tendency than heretofore to consider the laws of Mendel. Let us devote a brief study to Mendel and Mendelism.

Gregor Johann Mendel (1822-1884) was Abbot of Brunn, and he propounded the theory that plants had certain well-marked individual features; in other words he suggested (and proved by demonstration) that they have "definite and separate unit characters."

Does this suggest anything abstruse? Surely not. Men have "definite and separate unit characters," and why not plants?

As examples of characters in a Sweet Pea there are round seeds and wrinkled seeds, light seeds and dark seeds.

Mendel made numerous experiments with Peas, which he defined for character-units as (*a*) tall and dwarf; (*b*) yellow-seeded and green-seeded; (*c*) round-seeded and wrinkled-seeded.

The next thing that Mendel found—and it was a discovery of vast importance—was that these characters were separable in certain fixed proportions, and that when they had been separated they could be made to keep separate by selection.

For example, crossing a tall variety with a dwarf one, he could get both tall and dwarf, get them in the first place in certain fixed proportions, and in the course of three years get the dwarf plants fixed unalterably as dwarfs.

The practical cross-fertiliser will say: "What is there extraordinary in that? I have done it repeatedly without applying any other laws than my own experience and judgment."

Not in three years—not without many years of selection and rogueing. Mendelism supplies a short cut.

Proceeding, let us take Mendel's experiment of crossing tall and dwarf varieties. No matter which was used as the female parent, he got the following result: *first generation*, all the progeny tall; *second generation*, 75 per cent. tall, and 25 per cent. dwarf (let the reader fix these proportions of 3 to 1 firmly in his mind—they are the core of Mendelism); *third generation of tall plants*, some tall, some dwarf; those that are tall in the third generation will always remain tall; *third generation of dwarf plants*, all true dwarf, and fixed as dwarf for ever.

Before we go any further let us digest the foregoing thoroughly. (1) The fact that the first generation (scientists apply the formula F^1 to this) gives tall plants shows that tallness is more influential than dwarfness; the former character predominates, the latter is set back or recessed. For this reason tall plants would be spoken of as Dominants, and dwarf ones as Recessives. (2) The dominating character has lost a part of its force in the second generation (F^2), but retains the supremacy in a fixed proportion of three to one (this never varies more than a trifle). (3) We note the remarkable fact that the Recessives are always true in the third generation.

Now let us resume. We have got our Recessives fixed in the third year, but not our Dominants. A proportion equal to that of the Recessives will be true talls, but a proportion twice as large will give about three-quarters tall and one-quarter dwarf, and so selection must go on with the Dominants until, by a process of elimination, the Recessives have been worked out.

In the case of Sweet Peas, the character of Colour will be the one which is of the greatest importance to the raiser.

Here are a few interesting points about Mendelism as applied to Sweet Peas:—

(1) Cross a tall Sweet Pea with a Cupid, and the former will always be Dominant.

(2) Cross a coloured Sweet Pea with a white, and the former will be Dominant (but it may not be the same colour as the variety used for the cross).

(3) If a flower has sterile anthers, but a normal stigma, the hybrids resulting from a cross will all be fertile in the first generation. It may be said, therefore, that fertility is Dominant and sterility Recessive. As would be expected, sterile flowers reappear in the second generation in the proportion of one to three.

(4) If two whites are crossed together the hybrids may come of the original colour—purple—in F^1. This is an interesting case of reversion.

(5) If two fixed parents are crossed, all the variations which the cross is capable of yielding appear in the second generation, and many of these are already fixed.

(6) If purple and red Sweet Peas are crossed, the purple is Dominant.

(7) If erect-standard and hooded-standard varieties are crossed, the former are Dominant.

(8) When red is crossed with white the red is Dominant.

(9) When blue is crossed with red blue is Dominant. (Thus a blue-red cross in 1910 would work out as follows: 1911 (F^1) all blue; 1912 (F^2) reappearance of red in the proportion of one to three, and in a perfectly fixed state, as far as redness is concerned, as 1913 (F^3) will prove; of the blues only half would be found fixed in 1913.)

(10) It is most important that in saving the seed of a hybrid, the seed of each plant should be kept separate, even if all look exactly alike. Cross-breds may appear to be identical and yet have quite different breeding properties.

(11) To finally sum up Mendelism, it is a process by which fertilisation is conducted in accordance with certain fixed laws based on the existence of definite factors. When it is applied one parent must be Dominant and the other Recessive; the factors of both parents must appear in the second generation, one must be fixed, and the other must be unfixed in the third generation.

I will conclude this fascinating subject by giving a short bibliography of Mendelism, for the benefit of those who would like to study it fully.

Bateson, W., *Mendel's Principles of Heredity.* Cambridge University Press.

Bateson, W., *The Methods and Scope of Genetics*. Cambridge University Press.

Cuthbertson, Wm., *Mendelism as applied to Sweet Peas*. The Sweet Pea Annual, 1909.

Mendel, G. J., *The Principles of Heredity*. Journal of the Royal Horticultural Society, August, 1901.

Punnett, R. C., *Mendelism*. Bowes & Bowes, Cambridge.

The Gardeners' Chronicle, July 24th, 1909. Coloured plate of Mendelian Heredity in Sweet Peas.

CHAPTER IV.

OF THE SEEDS OF SWEET PEAS AND THE RAISING OF PLANTS, WITH A WORD AS TO CUTTINGS.

Sunlight shines this dewy morn on pastures shorn, on ripened corn,
    Sunlight gleams far upon the hills;
The Woodbine scents the hedgerow where the scarlet berries glow,
    The soaring lark her joyous carol trills.
Sunlight shines this dewy morn, this scented morn, this singing morn,
    On the moorland, on the heather, on the rills,
The scythesman chants his roundel where the nodding poppies blow,
    And the golden corn the harvest wagon fills.

Sunlight shines this summer morn from Thames to Tweed, from Leith to Lorne,
    Sunlight strews the garden path with gold.
The bees hum round the arbour where the blue Clematis swings,
    And the hidden lovers' age-long tale is told.
Sunlight shines this merry morn, this fragrant morn, this flowery morn,
    On the fragrant ten-week Stock and Sunflower bold;
And the florist turns his footsteps, while in glad content he sings,
    To the garden where the last Sweet Peas unfold.

THESE little hard balls which we gather from the pods fill us with mixed feelings.

We go into the garden, and our steps lead us instinctively to the Sweet Peas. We have no sense of active volition. We are "drawn." The flowers are fading. Soon their beauty will have gone unless we take active steps to circumvent match-making nature, who is as eager as any old maid of the village to get young folk mated.

Do we want seeds, or do we want flowers? Reader, if you are of the gentler sex you want both. You want to eat your cake and have it. I know your adorable, impossible aspirations. But you cannot gather seed and continue to have good flowers from the same plants. Of course, I speak generally. An odd pod is another matter.

Here is a white. It carries fours. The flowers are gloriously waved, and of great substance. It is an hourly joy to gaze on this lovely variety, which, in compliment to your maiden aunt on your father's side (who has "means") you have named Aunt Letitia. You are constantly feeling an impulse to go and feast your eyes upon it. You get up early in the morning, you hurry over your meals and so run the risk of contracting dyspepsia, you jump up from a favourite book, merely to taste the rapture of gazing on your lovely novelty. A florist to whom you have shown it has gazed piercingly at it, and then made you "an offer for the stock."

The real Aunt Letitia is going to fade slowly out of life sterile, but the same fate cannot be allowed to overtake her floral namesake. (You do not, of course, commit the error of offending the maiden susceptibilities of your important relative by making such a comparison to her.) Sooner or later seed of the wonderful white must be saved, and yet the temptation to keep the plant growing and flowering for the sake of the pleasure which its flowers provide is almost irresistible. It is so easy to do—merely the regular picking of the flowers while young, regular watering, weekly soakings of liquid manure. July passes, August is half way through, the florist asks you how Aunt Letitia is podding when you meet him at a show, and you are driven to a contemptible evasion.

The time comes when a final decision must be made. Prolonged wet weather may set in, so endangering the harvest. You have to decide which course you will choose: maintain bloom until the latest moment, regardless of the seed, or get the best possible crop. Are your artistic or your commercial instincts the strongest? Or is it not a case of that at all, but of harsh necessity?

Mid-August! Is that really the latest? It is the very latest, if you wish to be on the safe side. Not a day longer can be granted to you. I am no stern, unsympathetic judge, and I do not pass this dread sentence callously. It is with real emotion that I don the black cap. Even now you may have to resort to the plan of withdrawing the roots from the ground, and leaving the plants suspended by the sticks. Seedsmen do this with late crops in a wet season, in order to bring growth to a standstill, and so permit seed-production to go on; but I cannot think that it should be done if avoidable.

Reluctantly you withdraw your hand from the waterpot. Tremblingly you beg your wife (who will flatly refuse to understand the necessity for it) to abstain from cutting Aunt Letitia for the rest of the season. Meekly you retire, under the chilling effects of her silent and icy displeasure, to a part of the house where you cannot see the Sweet Peas. Nature has her way with the plants. They " run to seed." Flowers form, are self-fertilised, and grow old. The stigma protrudes, a flattened green spear, from the keel. The petals fall. A slender green boat with the pistil curving up in front of it (really it rather reminds you of a gondola), is seen embedded in the green, five-winged calyx. It is the pod formed of the fused carpels, and it is covered with fine, silky white hairs. The ten stamens draggle limply around it, they " lag superfluous on the stage." The pod swells rapidly, and presently begins to shrivel; the seeds are ripe.

To get the best of seed we ought to have early ripening. I do not like the withdrawal of the plants to force on maturity. Let plants that are to yield seed mature naturally, on sap sent up by the roots. Get seed in July if possible, should Nature provide the conditions for it.

In the Spring-time we hear much discussion on the germination of Sweet Peas, and those who fail speculate as to whether the seed was " over-ripe " or " unripe " when it was gathered. Those who speak of " over-ripeness " are under the influence, probably, of seed which has a very hard, dark skin. Such seed may have ripened under precisely the same conditions as another variety to which they would never think of applying the term, because its skin is paler and softer. I do not see how a seed can be over-ripe. When it has ripened it is finished. Nor do I see how a seed can be unripe provided it matures under natural conditions. If the pods are gathered late in a wet season, while they are still soft and green, and are laid on a shelf to mature, the seed may not ripen.

It is always better to gather the pods singly as fast as they mature than to take up the plants, lay them in a heap, and thrash the seed out. The quantity of seed varies with the weather and variety. Spencers yield much less than old-type flowers. Professional seedsmen, who do not grow their plants strongly, consider two ounces per yard of row a fair crop of the former, and eight ounces of the latter.

Are you an amateur, my reader, who knows naught of seed except the buying and the sowing of it? Let me try and arouse your special interest in the subject of Sweet Pea seeds.

First, you notice that some seeds are dark in colour and some are nearly white. Varieties with white flowers generally have white seeds, but, strange to say, one stock of one of the older whites, Sadie Burpee, has black seed. Dark seeds have harder skins than light ones, as a rule. And here comes an opening for a little practical hint. If you are sowing different sorts of Sweet Peas in one box put the dark-seeded varieties near the centre, because the soil is likely to be moister than on the outsides. The light-seeded varieties can go into the positions which are likely to be driest and best drained. If dark-seeded varieties do not germinate at the outset, do not write an irate letter to the seedsman, declaring that the seed was bad, as, indeed you were convinced that it would prove to be from the first moment that you saw it, because it was small and shrivelled. Take a sharp knife, and, beginning at the tip, cut through the outer skin, and strip it off; then sow the seed again. If you should find a difficulty in removing the skin soak the seed in water for a few hours and then try a second time.

The seeds of Sweet Peas differ in shape as well as in colour. Most of the varieties have round, smooth seed; but some have small, mottled, wrinkled seed, which looks old and shrivelled from its birth. Many lavender, blue and mauve varieties, including Lady Grizel Hamilton, Frank Dolby, the Marquis, Romolo Piazzani, Mrs. Walter Wright, Dorothy Tennant and Mrs. Higginson, junior, have this class of seed. As a whole, they are certainly more liable to defective germination than the smooth-seeded sorts, and the grower must not expect quite so good a percentage of successes from them. But all the blues are not distinguished by this poor looking seed. Navy Blue, for instance, has normal seed.

The seed of many varieties, notably the thin-skinned, light-seeded ones, will often show a number of cracked or split specimens. Navy Blue generally includes a good many. Very little significance need be attached to them, but in view of the fact that they indicate that moisture penetrates the skin readily, the resolution should be made to avoid keeping the soil very wet.

The seed, as I have said, is an interesting organism. If you could dissect it, and examine it closely, you would find that it consisted of: (1) an outer coat (testa); (2) an inner coat (endopleura); (3) seed leaves (cotyledon); (4) incipient stem (plumule); (5) incipient root (radicle). (Fig. 5, p. 40). The stem and root can feed the plant between them when once they have got a start, but they need a send-off, and this the seed-leaves provide, as they are stored with sugar, starch and oil for that express purpose. When growth starts, under

ETTA DYKE.
The grand white waved variety. See Chapter XII.

To come to the point, when, where and how shall we sow Sweet Peas? Here are plain questions of great moment. I may assume that my readers will include the following classes: (1) Those who want very early flowers and have glass. (2) Those who want to win prizes (a) and have glass, (b) and have no glass. (3) Those who do not care for all the silver cups in existence, but want Sweet Peas in their gardens half the year.

(1) We want flowers early in May and we have glass. What must we do? We must sow in late summer or early autumn of the previous year. Our course is this: to sow about the end of September in boxes or small pots, and place the receptacles in a cold frame. Assuming that we sow in boxes, to put the plants singly in small sixties (3-inch pots) about a month after sowing. In any case to keep the plants in the frame until February. The compost may consist of three parts of fibrous loam, one part of leaf mould, and a tenth of coarse sand, and it may rest on crocks surfaced with moss or leaf-mould to provide drainage. There is one thing of the first importance, and that is to avoid keeping the soil sodden. If the soil is moist enough to feel damp when squeezed in the hand, and take the impression of the fingers lightly (but not, of course, like a lump of putty would) no water will be needed just after the seeds have been sown. The first and subsequent waterings should be given when the soil gets dry enough to begin to crack away from the sides. This will not happen very often during the winter.

A second matter of moment is shallow sowing. If the seeds are covered to a depth of half-an-inch it will be ample.

Air should be admitted to the frame during fine weather throughout the winter, but the lights had better be kept closed during heavy rains, hard frosts, or fog.

The nervous beginner will have many a harrowing moment during spells of severe winter weather, for he will imagine his poor little plants shrivelling up under the icy grip of Jack Frost. I hasten to assure him that, given comparative dryness of the soil, nothing whatever will happen to them; but if he will insist on swilling them with water day after day the worst visions that his horrified imagination can succeed in conjuring up may be exceeded by the reality.

I have spoken of an unheated frame, but a greenhouse will do, provided the pots are near the glass, and the house is unheated. A warm greenhouse will not do at all. It will rush the plants along, get them to an unwieldy size, and make them soft.

At the end of February the plants will be ready for a shift into 6-inch pots. They may remain in cool quarters until these pots are showing roots at the drainage hole, and then be shifted into 8 or 9-inch pots and put into a house with a temperature of 55° to 60°. Plenty of air, and water as the soil dries, will keep them hard and healthy. They will be three to five feet high by the end of April, and giving their first blooms on long stems.

(2) We do not want very early flowers, but we want to win prizes at the summer shows (*a*) we have glass; (*b*) we have no glass.

(*a*) We need not use our glass before February, but there is no harm in autumn sowing if we care to practise it, always provided that we keep the plants cool and dry. Many successful exhibitors sow under cool conditions in autumn. They

Fig. 6.—RAISING SWEET PEAS IN POTS.
Left side—Section of pot, showing seed sown.
Right side—Young plants resulting, ready to go out.

take care to keep the plants on the dry side, as then there is very little risk of injury from frost. In February the plants are small, but they are nicely rooted, and they can be put out in April or May with the certainty that—other things being right—they will go ahead rapidly and vigorously.

Generally speaking February is a good time to sow under glass. Plants from seed sown about mid-February will be ready for planting out in April. But the grower who is anxious to have new varieties must not delay placing his order with the seedsman until a few days before he proposes to sow. The stock of a particular variety may be short, in which case it may be exhausted before the New Year. To be quite on the safe side the seeds should be bought in autumn.

Five seeds may go equidistant round a well-drained 5-inch pot (Fig. 6) near the sides, and one may go in the middle.

A liberal admixture of leaf mould in the compost is advisable, because the roots bind round it well, and when the ball comes to be shaken out for planting purposes (with the soil moist, of course) the plants can be separated without the roots being bared. I sometimes put ten seeds in a 6-inch pot, and have no trouble in getting the plants apart. If there are plenty of 3-inch pots available one seed may be sown in each, there is then no risk of check through separation.

The plants will be all right in the pots without sticks until they are about five inches high, but after that they will begin to form tendrils, and should have twigs stuck among them if the weather does not permit of their being planted out. They will extend more rapidly if they stand at some distance from the glass than if they are close to it, and as slow extension is desirable it is wise to keep them close to the glass.

The pots ought to stand on a base of cinders because earthworms and wireworms are checked. Without the cinders the former might establish themselves in the soil and the latter feed on the seeds.

(b) It is a handicap to be without glass in raising plants for exhibition. The shows begin in July, and the plants ought to be strong enough to start flowering (and producing long stems, too) by the end of June. It will be quite possible to get plants equal to this from outdoor sowings if the district is mild, the soil rich, and the treatment correct; but I do not think that it could be relied on everywhere. Cannot those of us who garden in "late-Spring" districts manage a small cold frame? Let us try. It will only cost a few shillings, and it will be a great comfort both to the plants and ourselves. If we must sow out of doors let us take special precautions to make our soil rich and mellow. Let us keep a very sharp look out for slugs, and let us take precautions against wireworms. (See chapter XI.)

What about Autumn sowing out of doors in localities where the springs are cold and the soil poor? Will not this give the plants a good start? There is the risk to consider in the case of expensive novelties. If you buy Sweet Pea seeds at the rate of five for a shilling you are naturally reluctant to expose them to all the dangers of a winter in the ground. Try some cheaper varieties first, and if the result is satisfactory extend the plan. When autumn-sowing out of doors is practised it will be wise to make the soil very friable, if necessary by adding road grit, burnt rubbish, mortar rubbish, leaf mould or potting shed sweepings. Further, to sprinkle some sea-sand well permeated with broken shell in the drills under and over the seed. Two inches will be a suitable depth to cover the latter. When the plants are through sprinkle some more of the sand around them. Late September and early October is a good time for sowing.

The earliest time at which it is safe to sow out of doors in the New Year must depend upon the soil, situation and weather. February sowing will be safe, provided: (1) the soil is friable and moist, but not sodden; (2) the situation is not exposed to cold winds; (3) the weather is dry and mild. Use sea sand as before; if it is difficult to get use crushed oyster shell, which many manure dealers supply.

It is the rule in sowing out of doors to "allow for losses." My old friend, Jem Apps, is great on this. He has all the mistrust and caution of his class. "They varmints" (by this collective phrase he describes all creeping, crawling and flying enemies of seeds and seedlings), "they varmints 'll have some of 'em, dew what yew may; better 'low for it without no more argumenting." This is the sowing philosophy of a cottage gardener with thirty years' experience behind him. It leads him to his crowning sin—thick sowing—an evil from which he has never attempted to free himself, and never will. He sows a pint of garden Peas to ten yards of drill. He sows Sweet Peas at the rate of a dozen to the square inch. He will not see that if he wins prizes it is in spite of this, not because of it. He wins because he competes with others of his class who commit the same mistake, but who are a little less thorough than Jem himself in the preparation of their soil, and not so "cunning" in choosing the right moment for sowing.

A Cornish grower of my acquaintance "goes the whole hog" in the matter of thin sowing. "You plant six inches apart, don't you? Very well, sow six inches apart." And he does! No half measures here. Celtic courage rampant. Slugs? Sea-sand. Ground-pests? Sea sand. Birds? Wire. There you have it in brief.

We are not of the exhibitor class, perhaps; we merely want a nice display in the garden? Ah, how happy we! No worry to get our plants forward, no anxiety to have flowers by a certain day, no midnight spectres in the way of colossal slugs creeping over our bodies, no early morning scrambles across country to catch trains running at unearthly hours, no all-night vigils in exhibition tents, no breakfastless mornings, no horrible fourth prize cards where we were sure of firsts! We are not so foolish as to feel envious when we go into Jenkins's dining-room and see a huge silver cup on his sideboard. We think of the dozen exhibitors who were absolutely sure of annexing that cup, and whose sideboards are now worse than empty. We are unheroic, we are made of common clay, we are even pusillanimous, if you like. But we have a good time with our Sweet Peas all the same.

There are two sides to the showing question. Suppose that Jenkins was forced by circumstances to leave that deep loam of his and go and live on an exposed hillside with six inches of poor, fibreless soil over chalk, would he still be in a position to "lift the cup"? No, he would not, and his wisest policy would be to recognise the fact, save himself mortification, and when people remarked that they noticed he was not exhibiting now, respond: "The wife got tired of my being away so much," or something equally facile.

Some of us might spend our last halfpenny, give up every moment of our time, take all the measures that skill could devise, and never have the ghost of a chance of winning an important competition. No prudent general would fight with his right wing commanded by a hill and his base in a gravel pit. He would either find a better position, or retreat.

When we put aside all considerations of showing we can sow Sweet Peas with a delightful sense of irresponsibility. We can sow when and where we like. It is quite probable that we shall sow a row of mixed seed, or of a few inexpensive varieties, out of doors, in Autumn. Certainly we shall sow outside in Spring. We will not, however, be outdone in judgment by any number of Jem Appses. We shall prepare our land by irreproachable methods—digging two spades deep if the ground will allow of it on some selected occasion in the Winter when the soil crumbles freely, putting a good coat of manure under the top spit, leaving the surface rough to be crumbled down by the weather, and sowing in Spring when the soil is moist enough and friable enough to fall into a fine tilth. (See Chapter V.)

If we lack courage enough to put our seeds six inches apart we must compromise in one of two ways: (1) by dropping clusters of three seeds each at six-inch intervals along the drill, and thinning the resulting plants down to the best one; (2) by sprinkling the seeds in thinly, and pulling out the surplus ones when we are sure that we have a good stock of plants to choose from.

There is one thing that we must not do, and that is sow thickly. Generally speaking, we can do as we like when we are not growing for show, but in this matter we are bound by the rules of good culture, and must not disobey.

But are seeds the only method of propagation? Can we not raise plants from cuttings? Yes, the two-inch tips of young plants raised from seed in winter can be inserted in sandy soil and placed under a bell-glass or hand-light in a warm greenhouse, but they must be protected from sunlight or they will certainly "go off." If kept shaded they ought to root inside a fortnight. Directly they begin to grow they should have light and air. The tips can be taken off and struck in turn, like blue bedding Lobelias.

CHAPTER V.

OF THE BEST SOIL AND MANURES FOR SWEET PEAS.

>You kiss your love by the pale moonlight,
>And you dream sweet dreams while the stars are bright;
>You tread the paths of a spirit land,
>Where the white shapes wander hand in hand.
>The morning comes, and she's fresh and fair
>As the sunlight gleams in her golden hair;
>But you see that the spirit dream's a sham
>When she makes short work of a plate of ham.

I WOULD gladly believe, if I could, that all these fair flowers of ours grow best with no sustenance but pure air and pure water. It seems degrading to associate such beautiful and fragrant things with heaps of unsightly and smelly manure, the refuse of coarse animal existence. But facts have to be faced. We know that Sweet Peas will grow to a certain standard in unmanured soil, but experience teaches us that they rarely give of their best except when they are highly fed.

There are some favoured folk who rejoice in a soil that will grow almost every kind of plant well without liberal manuring. Perhaps it is a substantial red or brown loam, many feet deep. They plant Apples—the trees grow freely, and their dark polished branches are free from the slightest trace of canker. They form a Strawberry bed, and in a year the plants are laden with luscious fruit. They make a Rose garden—the pillars are covered with vigorous growths and brilliant bunches of flowers within a few months. In such a soil Sweet Peas will grow strongly and bear large, brilliant flowers on stems eighteen inches long. There are Sweet Peas for week on week. The garden is gay with them. The vases are full of them.

How many of you enjoy such a soil, my readers? Ayes to the right, and Noes to the left: the Noes have it. Many us of have seen such a soil in some turn or other of our garden wanderings, and have gazed at it enviously, covetously. It has filled us with longing. We are so eager to give our flowers the best of everything that if a surreptitious knock over the head, delivered judiciously while the owner was stooping to gather up a sample, would have put us in possession of it, we should have administered the blow. Or perhaps a dexterous dab on the solar plexus—but these speculations are wholly vain. Where soil is concerned we cannot hit, grab and run.

It is an exasperating trait in many writers about flowers to tell us that the particular plants on which they are expatiating do best in such-and-such a soil, and there leave the matter. The assumption is that everyone of us is the owner of a dozen large estates, and if we have not the right soil on one of them we transfer a few truckloads from another. The truth is that we have to do the best we can with the one garden that circumstances place at our disposal. If the soil is not what it should be we have to try and make it so with the aid of tools and manure.

The Sweet Pea is not really an exacting plant. It does not demand one kind of soil, and inflexibly refuse to thrive in all others. Do we not see it in every other cottage garden that we pass, whatever county we may happen to be in? And does not that mean that it is succeeding in soils of many different kinds? If the deep loam is the best, perhaps the thin, fibreless soil just above chalk is the worst, and that is not absolutely hopeless. There are many stages between the two extremes. There is the solid, uncompromising clay, which is apt to get pasty in winter, and must be left alone for weeks together; but which may crack badly in summer. A grim, dour soil this, but a soil of substantial merit. It is a soil rich in potash, tenacious of moisture. Sweet Peas may bloom late in it, but the odds are that they will bloom long. It is a soil that will always strain your muscles and often worry you, but in the end you will grow to like it, and will part from it with regret. The way to deal with this soil is to work it two or three spades deep during a dry spell in late Winter, and weave in a liberal dressing of manure between each two layers ("spits") of soil. If eighteen inch stems will satisfy you, bastard trench—that is, take off the top spit, turn over the bottom spit and, after putting on a coat of manure four inches thick, replace the top spit. But if nothing less than two feet stems will suffice, with four large flowers on each, and if the plants are to go on yielding exhibition blooms all the summer, trench deeper. Take off two spits and break up the third; with garden rubbish worked into the bottom spit, and a coat of manure laid on it, the way is prepared for replacing the middle spit. A coat of manure put on this makes a rich bed for the top spit.

I say that this should be done during a dry spell in Winter, and I entreat the cultivator to guard against doing it while the soil is very wet, or covered with snow. Such conditions mean a terrible mess for him or his workmen, and what is worse, a possible drying of the soil into stiff lumps, which no tool can crumble. It will not be found that the soil crumbles to powder on the surface even in the dry spell, nor is it desirable that it should; but it will fall into small lumps mingled with "crumb." Four pounds of superphosphate and half-a-pound of sulphate of iron may be mixed with some wood ashes from the garden fire and spread on each square rod of ground, then the whole surface will crumble down and can be raked fine and level in readiness for sowing and planting. The clay will be brought into such condition by this treatment that it will carry the plants up into lofty and spreading masses, and will keep them fresh and growing until the end of Autumn. Watering will rarely, if ever, be needed. Liquid manure need only be supplied for special purposes, such as the production of show flowers at a given date. With regular hoeing the surface can be kept loose and the under soil moist even through weeks of drought.

Let us take another class of soil—a light, sandy loam, perhaps overlying gravel. This is more easily worked than clay, and is open to cultivation over a longer period of the Winter; but it will want more help through the Summer. The trenching should be done in Autumn instead of Winter, and the coats of manure may be six inches deep instead of four—so much for a start. The following mixture of chemical manure may be laid on in February, the quantities given being per square rod: two pounds of sulphate of potash, one pound of steamed bone flour, three pounds of superphosphate, and half-a-pound of sulphate of iron. With a fair rainfall in Summer this feeding will suffice, but if the weather is dry soakings of liquid manure may be given weekly, and a mulch of manure may be spread along the rows.

The source and character of the liquid manure? If we are on a drainage system one source of supply is practically closed to us, save for a few secret contributions from the house, that delicacy deprives of a name. But where sewage is available it should be used, broken down with water if dark and rich. A neck-or-nothing amateur of my acquaintance has no half measures with the contents of his cesspool. Recalling the horror of the Highlander when he caught some abandoned wretches watering the whisky, he uses it neat, beginning when the plants are two inches high and continuing till they are eight feet. Prophecies of disaster through feeding too early dismay him for the nonce, but twenty-four hours later the clank of his pump tells that the old Adam is moving again.

Failing sewage, let us remember, if we are country dwellers, that a shilling has a highly stimulating effect on a village boy, and if we select the shepherd's son he will be permitted to start upon a quest for the dark diamonds of the meadows that may give us a substantial bag to soak in our tub, adding richness to a liquid which a bag of soot has already darkened.

Always, too, we have available those special fertilisers which find their way on to the market by two stages; the first, successful feeding experiments by a great exhibitor; the second, commercial mixing and putting up in tins of the chosen food for offer in the seed catalogue by a dealer. One is called, perhaps, "Moody's Sweet Pea Fertiliser." No need to ask who Moody is. Have we not all gazed with admiration and delight on the wonderful flowers which he has set up at a score of shows? Startup (of Startup's Lightning Seeds) does not tell us in so many words, on that page of his seed catalogue which contains an illustration of a tin of the Fertiliser, that Moody's wonderful success is due absolutely, entirely and unequivocally to the use of the Fertiliser, because he has to reserve a share for the quality of his (Startup's) seeds. But we are to understand that with Moody's Fertiliser and Startup's seeds we are on a sure road to equal success.

The luckless owner of what has been described as the worst soil for Sweet Peas—the thin, fibreless soil over chalk—may wonder if he is left irretrievably in the cold. No, but he must seek success by a different road, and be satisfied with a more modest share of it. If he should be breaking up meadow he will be sorely tempted to work in the turf, for the sake of its valuable fibre, and for the greater depth which it imparts. Without it what is there? A few inches of greyish dust as fibreless as sand. But what of leather jacket grubs and wireworm? They will be turned under if the turf is buried, and they will come up in thousands, eager, voracious, unappeasable. A long, wearying, costly battle will then begin—a battle which will assuredly harass the amateur severely, and may dishearten him completely.

On the whole I would not turn in the turf; I would stack it to rot down into potting soil. With it I should remove the greater quantity of the two arch-enemies. A season under Potatoes would further reduce them. When Autumn came six solid inches of rich decayed horse manure should go on to the surface, and after lying for a few weeks, should be turned in. Blending with the soil, it would impart body and humus. With a similar dressing the following year, and the turning in of any garden refuse, the soil would be considerably deepened and enriched. If there was still much trouble from ground pests a crop of Mustard could be sown and turned in green. It would harry the grubs and, rotting down, add further to the store of humus.

More water and liquid manure would be called for on the chalk than on the clay. Summer mulching with manure would be helpful, if not actually essential. In the suggestion that the soil might be improved by breaking up the chalk to the depth of a foot, and incorporating manure with it, I acquiesce; but I hardly dare ask the average amateur to undertake so laborious a task over a large area of ground; although I have it done myself. Each grower must decide for himself whether the end justifies the labour and expense.

There are soils which differ from the standards that I have treated on, and I may say of them collectively with perfect safety that they will be made the more suitable for Sweet Peas the more deeply they are cultivated and the more liberally they are manured.

One may feed with chemical fertilisers for special objects, such as the stimulation of plants that are attacked by fungi, and to encourage seed production. There are growers who never use natural manure for Sweet Peas, and get healthy plants, good flowers, and a bountiful harvest of seed.

If an amateur finds that his plants grow very slowly, from no external cause, and have a pinched look, he may (especially if plants here and there go off altogether) suspect a root enemy. A stimulus from some quick-acting fertiliser, such as nitrate of soda, nitrate of potash or phosphate of potash, given promptly, may carry the plants over the critical stage, and send them on into rapid, healthy growth. Only weak applications should be given. If the weather is wet an ounce of the fertiliser may be spread along each yard of row, half on each side, and pointed just under the surface. If dry, an ounce may be stirred into a gallon of water, and this quantity used to every yard of row or clump.

A wet season brings with it a great deal of the Pea mould. A purely potash fertiliser, such as sulphate of potash, supplemented by a modicum of sulphate of iron—say one ounce of the former and half-an-ounce of the latter per yard—will fortify the plants. And the wet season is bad for the seedsman, whose flowers often go off without podding. The fertilisers just named will help him, too, if pointed in during showery weather in early summer.

CHAPTER VI.

OF THE METHODS OF PLANTING AND SUPPORTING SWEET PEAS.

Peas along the border, Peas upon the lawn,
Peas against an eastern wall to welcome in the dawn,
Peas among the Roses, Peas behind the Pinks,
Peas to catch the western glow when evening sunlight sinks.
Oh, merry, merry, merry are the gay Sweet Peas,
Plant them where and how you will it's certain they will please.

Peas held up with Chestnut, Peas held up with Ash,
Peas asprawl on Hazel spray, Peas on larchen brash,
Peas on stiff unyielding wire, Peas tied up with string,
Peas upon the trellis work where the Rambler Roses swing.
Oh merry, merry, merry are the gay Sweet Peas,
Stake them when and how you will it's certain they will please.

IT is no ordinary task, this of planting the Sweet Peas. We do not set about it in the casual, perfunctory way in which we proceed to stick in a bundle of Cabbages. There is no such thing as seizing the nearest dibber, making a plunge, a jab, and then going on to the second plant without so much as looking at the first. The methods employed in marshalling a Sunday School treat are not those for the royal nursery.

Our newest Sweet Pea may be as strong, as sturdy, as well-rooted as a plant from the commonest mixture, but our interest in it is so profound, our anxiety about it so intense, that we handle it with a care which approaches fondling. We are almost afraid to trust it out of doors, lest some hateful slug should fall upon it and eat it up.

Sooner or later this weakness has to be overcome, and it helps us to conquer it if we are able to survey a well prepared soil. Those roomy spaces in the border, those circles on the edge of the lawn, those long trenches—all with the soil standing up in a mellow, crumbly mass above the surrounding level—do they not inspire confidence? Do they not invite us to hurry up with our planting so that they can show us what they can do? Do they not stimulate our imagination, and prompt us to conjure up pictures of lofty columns all aglow with bloom? Do they not whisper to us of two-feet stems, of huge flowers borne in fours ? Do we not see through the dining-room window the glitter of a silver Challenge Vase, won in strenuous fight at the Puddlebury Sweet Pea Show ?

We spared no trouble in preparing our ground, and now its time has come. It has to prove what it can do. It has to show what is in it. April is here. There have been pleasant showers, and the surface lumps fall to pieces beneath the rake. We have sturdy plants in pots, showing by the formation of tendrils and the protrusion of roots at the drainage that they are eager for a move on.

Have we been thorough with our seedlings ? Have we shifted them from the seed pots, and put them singly in small pots ? If so, our planting task is easy. With the soil moist in the pots, so that it may not fall away from the roots at the slightest disturbance, we have only to invert the pot, tap the edge, lift it off, and we have a complete entity—a plant with a mass of roots entwined in a symmetrical ball of loam. We plunge the trowel into the soil, and it sinks deep into the unctuous, unresisting mass. We withdraw it, charged with soil, and a capacious hole is revealed. Lovingly we place in the ball, lingeringly we press the soil around it, leaving a shallow basin round the collar, so that any water which is given may gurgle down to the very heart of the roots. The whole process is easy and pleasant, and directly it is done our fears fall away. The plant looks happy, it is in its rightful element. As for slugs, some freshly slaked quicklime dusted along will keep them at a distance.

Need it be said that we plant thinly, whether we are forming rings or rows ? If our soil is deep and rich we put our plants not an inch less than a foot apart ; and even if it is poor we do not crowd, we give six inches.

Some of us may have grown two seedlings together in a four or five-inch pot. The planting out of these is easy, too. We remove the pot, carve straight through the ball with a bold stroke as in cutting cheese, and divide it into halves, each with its own roots, each almost as homogeneous as the single plants.

It is when we have sown several seeds in one five or six-inch pot that the need for circumspection comes. With the most careful and skilful handling a certain amount of root disturbance is inevitable. The roots have probably become rather entangled, and must be separated delicately, or they will be broken. But with care no injury ensues. We keep a little soil with each plant, we squeeze it round the roots so that they cannot get dry, and we plant promptly. If the plants have to remain in the pots until they threaten to become entangled, the task of planting will be simplified by placing twigs among the plants (Fig. 7).

Fig. 7.—Plants must not be kept in pots after this stage unless twigs are put in to support them.

Thereafter we have the daily delight of watching the plants grow. At first they move slowly, because they are "getting established," to use a gardener's phrase. They are making fresh roots. They are getting hold of the soil. No hurrying them, please. No soaking with water, unless the soil is very dry. No liquid manure. Just let things take their course. Keep lime near them always, for the slug is ever watchful.

It is easy to see when the great move has come. You see the thickening of the stem, the expansion of the leaves, the flinging out of tendrils. It is almost as though we had a seedling one day and a plant the next. And so comes the staking.

It has long been a belief of mine that Peas grow the better, even when young and without tendrils, for having sticks near them. Before you dismiss this as hopelessly fanciful, study the plants for a year or two. I am credulous enough to believe that a plant knows whether it has a support near it or not. And I think that it throws out tendrils the sooner for knowing that there is something for them to cling to. We all have our little weaknesses. You may believe in palmistry and dialogues with the dead. I will humour you, and you must humour me.

If there is an objection to putting big sticks to little Peas (every amateur who has a wife knows that he is liable to admonishment on this score), compromise by chopping twigs from the pile of sticks that is lying in the yard, and putting them near the plants; they will be much better than nothing. But let there be no nonsense about doing the final staking in good time.

How shall we support our Sweet Peas? What material shall we use, and how shall we use it? Our broad choice is between (1) sticks, (2) wire. If we are amateurs we shall probably choose sticks of some kind, if trade growers we may use wire.

In the country, Pea sticks cost from fourpence to sixpence per bundle of twenty-five. They may be Chestnut, or Ash, or Hazel or Larch, according to the planting of the nearest woodland. We must allow a bundle to every four yards. The ends must be sharpened in order to facilitate the forcing down of the sticks deep enough to make them firm with a minimum of disturbance to the roots. Do not let us skimp our sticks. If we trench our ground two or three feet deep it will be strange if we do not get plants six feet high, and we may get them nine. Old sticks are not much use in these circumstances, for they are generally short as well as brittle. The few shillings we save by them in spring we are quite likely to lose in summer, for the plants may blow over in stormy weather, and demand a considerable expenditure of time and material before they will consent to look heavenward again.

The village coal merchant, or haulier, or farmer, or forester, who quotes for the sticks, will always give of his best material if he knows what it is for. He is just as much a slave of the Sweet Pea as the cashier at the bank who shovels gold about with such nonchalance, or the invoicing clerk in your office, who dons a silk hat so much smarter than yours when closing time comes. He will very likely prove to have more than a passing acquaintance with the best varieties, and may even have a sport of his own which he is trying to fix. You will humour him in these matters, so long as you get tall sticks with plenty of spray. In clumps we may have stakes and string (Fig. 8).

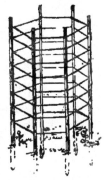

Fig. 8.—Stakes and string for supporting clumps of Sweet Peas.

The amateur who looks to the quality of his flowers generally fights shy of wire. He has a fear of the blossoms beating against it in windy weather, and getting badly cut. The seed grower, who does not want exhibition flowers, often employs galvanised wire netting. He uses it of large mesh for the sake of economy and about six feet high, mounted on stout stakes or iron rods. He will tell you that the first cost is greater than that of the sticks, but that it is more quickly set up, thereby effecting a saving in labour, that it can be rolled up and stored away at the end of the season, and that it will last for several years.

Galvanised wire frames are sometimes pressed into service. If might be thought that these can only be used for straight rows, but that is quite wrong. They can be bent round into a circle, tied, and used for clumps. Are you growing clumps eight or nine feet high? Then get, if you like, a pair of four feet high wire frames for each, fasten each in a circle, mount one on the top of the other, fasten them securely to strong uprights, and you have a splendid support.

Several good patent wire supports for Sweet Peas are now on the market, notably Sydenham's Ladder (Fig. 9) and Smith & Fletcher's Collapsible. These are a great convenience to growers in districts where sticks are difficult to get.

Let us not forget expanding trellis work, so often sniffed at as "suburban," and yet so cheap and useful. Do you want to hide some unsightly object quickly? Call trellis work and Sweet Peas to your aid, and the thing is done. A few weeks, and you have a glorious screen of foliage and flowers.

And do not let us forget that Sweet Peas, like Scarlet Runners, can be supported with simple string, as one of the photographic illustrations shows.

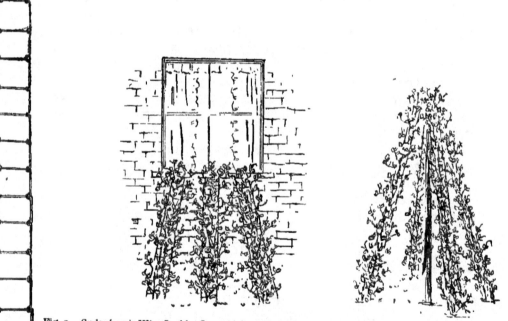

Fig. 9.—Sydenham's Wire Ladder Support for Sweet Peas, which may be fixed on a central pole or against a wall. The "ladder" folds up into a very small compass when not in use.

CHAPTER VII.

OF THE PLACES IN WHICH SWEET PEAS MAY BE GROWN; HOW THEY MAY BE USED IN BEDS AND HERBACEOUS BORDERS, AND ON WALLS AND FENCES.

There are Phloxes in my borders, there are Pinks along the edge
(Mrs. Sinkins curtseys humbly while Her Majesty I pledge);
There are Roses on my arches, there's Clematis on my wall,
But the gay and dancing Sweet Pea is the fairest of them all.

The Daffodils a-quiver chase the sunlight from their bed,
(The heralds sound the trumpets with the Empress at their head)
The Tulips lift their massy cups, the Iris lights its torch,
But my dearest love comes homeward, to the Sweet Peas by the porch.

Lofty Larkspurs stand on duty, loyal blue-clad sentinels,
The Madonna Lilies near them open wide their snow-white bells,
The sun-warmed Poppies shimmer, the sweet Carnations glow,
But still my eyes, love-brightened, to the nodding Sweet Peas go.

THE earliest recollections of Sweet Peas are the same with all of us—a mixed row in a cottage garden, fluttering gaily above the Snapdragons and Cloves. It is not the same village, nor the same cottage, but the row of Sweet Peas is the same. In one case it was the widow Grimes who grew them—she who shrilled invective at the village boys as they passed on their way to school, on the ground that they threw stones at her door—a thing which no happy English child has ever been known to do. In another it was Billy Chandler, who had a club foot and walked with a stick—a knobbly stick which he was wont to hurl violently at anybody who annoyed him, in reckless disregard of the liability of its coming back again. In a third it was Dotty Pridgeon, the natural, whose brain had been turned at seeing his little brother drowned in the mill pond, and who talked to his flowers in an unceasing mumble which nobody understood, but which the Sweet Peas knew perfectly well.

The Widow Grimes always insisted on exhibiting Sweet Peas at the village show. She never won a prize, because she always acted in flagrant opposition to the terms of the schedule. When it stipulated for nine bunches of flowers, the Widow Grimes put in twelve. When the Committee raised the number to twelve she put in nine. In each case she told the judges exactly what she thought of them afterwards. She also gave the officers an unvarnished prophecy as to the blight that might be expected to rest upon their families for many generations for their wicked treatment of her.

We see Sweet Peas grown in all sorts of ways nowadays, but we never see a more charming floral picture than the cottage rows that we used to love in byegone days. In truth, Sweet Peas never look so thoroughly happy and light-hearted as when growing in a mixed row. It is as though they had no cares of state, no thoughts of convention, to worry them. They have no question of deportment to weigh. They would as lief wear their sweethearts' hats as their own. Every day is Bank Holiday with them, every place is Hampstead Heath, and every concertina is a Viennese Band.

We specialise Sweet Peas so much in these days that we are apt to forget how truly delightful mixed rows are—real mixed rows, mind, not rows made up of blocks of separate varieties without any regard to the association of colours.

Please do not think me inconsiderate. Do not, in reproachful accents, charge me with luring you on to take an interest in named varieties, and then bidding you give up all your scanty space to a mixture at twopence per ounce. Let me tell you what you can do—what I myself am bent on doing "if I am spared" (this was the opening phrase of the Widow Grimes's last speech to me, in which she told me what she was going to do to Jemmie Briggs for thrusting a homeless and decrepit cat into her pantry window) if I am spared until next spring. No more of those higgledy-piggledy blocks of sorts. No more hotch-potches of colour. Two things shall I try, and you, reader, can do likewise. The first is to have a row of varieties in separate blocks, carefully associated as to colour. The second, to have a row of named varieties mixed in short blocks.

Here is my first plan:

| Mauve. | Red. | White. | Pink. | Blue. | Cream. |

My mauve will not be a common mauve, my red a poor red, my white an indifferent white. The first will be the famous Duchess of Battersea, the second the popular Ruritania

BEDS AND BORDERS, WALLS AND FENCES. 59

Rival, the third the charming Marylebone Maid—unless, indeed, these varieties have been superseded between the writing of this book and the publication of its tenth edition next spring.

Here is my second plan:

Mauve. Red. White.	Pink. Blue. Cream.

Observe, the same colours, the same varieties, but they are mixed in the blocks instead of being separate. I shall put a label near each group with the name of each of the three varieties on it. The colours are quite distinct. I shall have them attached to their names in my garden book, and so I cannot confuse them.

I believe that I shall like the effect of the second scheme best. The colours will help each other better in the more intimate association. So convinced do I feel of this, and so probable do I think it that many readers will think so too, that I am encouraged to offer more suggestions for mixed colour blocks, and here they are:

Salmon Light Blue.	Rose. Light Blue.	Salmon. Pink. Cream.	Cream. Light Blue.

All these blends look well.

With this scheme we get the advantage of beautiful colour associations in combination with the interest of growing special varieties under names. Although it does not appear to have occurred to anybody to mix their named Sweet Peas, there is no real objection to it, provided the proper colours are associated. And they need not be mixed in rectangles alone, they can be mixed in circles.

Sometimes the seedsman provides us with a mixture where he should supply distinct sorts. We buy John Startup and Sons' famous novelty, Horatio Nelson Startup, under the assurance that it is a "magnificent waved Gentian Blue, of the largest size, bearing fours, an equally fine garden and show variety, absolutely fixed." We pay a shilling for six seeds, we devote hours of care and attention to the seedlings, we get frantic at the sight of every slug, and when at last we feel that the plants are safe we tell our friends of the treasure which we possess and await the flowering with eager expectancy. Picture our horror, our rage, our despair, when Horatio Nelson Startup presents us with a wide range of colours, not one of which gives us the faintest reminder of the bounding main. Our beautiful colour scheme is smashed to smithereens, and in its place we have a "colour cacophony," which gives us dreadful shocks.

How can we guard against a catastrophe such as this? We must do one thing above all others, and that is, abstain from putting into our colour scheme any novelty which does not carry an award from the National Sweet Pea Society. There is no fear of overlooking the fact of such an award having been made; the seedsman who is lucky enough to get it will not put it in small type in an out-of-the-way corner of his list. And the Society will not make it unless it has strong evidence that the variety is true.

I do not go so far as to suggest that we should decline to buy novelties altogether unless they have the award, and Sweet Pea lovers would not take any notice of me if I did. Of course we will buy Sweet Pea novelties, out of the interest which we feel in the flower, and our desire to keep level with our neighbours, and to give us something to wait, and watch, and hope for. But we will not risk them in our precious art scheme without good evidence of their fixity. We will grow them separately, either tacked on to other novelties in a row, or in clumps.

By adopting the clump system of growing Sweet Peas we can introduce our favourite flower into beds and borders, where straight rows could not be accommodated. And the clumps may be of one variety only, or of certain colour blends. In this connection we have to think of the permanent occupants of the beds and borders.

Hardy herbaceous perennials are the core of many flower gardens nowadays. We make wide borders for them, prepare the ground generously, and plant the finest kinds, taking care to arrange the colours so that they make pleasing harmonies. There is no muddle-planting. We do not fling the plants in pell-mell, thinking only of "filling up." We group the plants in relation to height and colour. We rigorously avoid crowding. In such well-arranged borders Sweet Peas can often be accommodated with advantage. Let me tell you of one or two ways in which they can be used, and make a strong addition to the charm of the border.

(1) A clump of primrose Sweet Peas may be set between a clump of lilac Goat's Rue (*Galega*) and metallic blue Sea Holly (*Eryngium*).

BEDS AND BORDERS, WALLS AND FENCES.

(2) A red Sweet Pea may stand beside a mauve Michaelmas Daisy, and have a clump of white Chrysanthemums (Ox-eye Daisies) in front of it.

(3) We may set a clump of cream Sweet Peas near a group of blue Delphiniums.

(4) We may form a lovely group with the salmon Sweet Pea Henry Eckford (or Earl Spencer, or Nancy Perkin) the Rose Mallow (*Lavatera*—also an annual), and a yellow Hollyhock or Chrysanthemum.

(5) Slightly varying (4) we may set a clump of salmon-coloured Sweet Peas each side of a pillar of Dorothy Perkins Rose, and put a group of Horace Martin Chrysanthemum in front. (All of these will be in bloom in September, if the Sweet Peas are kept picked, and the position is one that does not get all the midday and afternoon sun.)

You do not object to a Rose pillar in a herbaceous border I hope? Believe me, it is very much at home there. Let it be of Larch, with the bark on, if possible, for then it will be straight, and such patches of bark as show through the rosy clusters and twining greenery of the Rose (but there will not be many) will have a pleasant bronzy hue.

Sweet Pea people sometimes argue as to the respective merits of the row and clump system of growing Sweet Peas. An advocate of the latter will say it is the better because the sun gets round the plants more thoroughly than it can round rows. There is not much in this. Very few amateurs grow Sweet Peas largely enough to need several parallel rows, and those who do know quite well how necessary it is to keep the rows sufficiently far apart to insure sunshine. Frankly, I think the plants do equally well in either rows or clumps. It is a matter of the convenience of the grower.

Clumps of Sweet Peas look charming on lawns. They should be a little to the left or right of the principal windows if there is a view; if not, they may be arranged dead in front to form a screen. If they grow very strongly in a rich soil and a humid climate, running to eight or ten feet high, they may be supported by taking two galvanised wire frames four feet high and eight feet long for each clump, bending them round into circles and tying them, then setting one on top of the other, as described on pages 56-7. A couple of long, stout stakes, well driven down, will keep them in position. Ordinary Pea sticks will suffice for clumps five to seven feet high.

The owner of a very small garden will not exclude Sweet Peas as too bulky for him. He will form rings a yard across at six-feet intervals along his flower border, and either sow

Sweet Peas thinly in them, or set plants six inches apart. No garden is too small to accommodate a few clumps of Sweet Peas, grown thus.

One thinks of the small suburban gardener in connection with growing Sweet Peas on walls and fences. He has only a small strip of soil round the division between his own garden and his neighbour's, the centre of the garden being taken up with the grass plot. Shall the grass plot be sacrificed? Perish the thought! Where shall the bairns frisk and gambol if the whole of the garden be given up to flowers, bordered by narrow paths, off which the children may not stray under pain of awful penalties? We will make the most of this border, and if we do but manure it well, and work it deeply, we shall achieve a very tolerable success.

From one suburban garden that I sometimes visit I see in another an earnest youth of twenty or thereabouts pursuing the cult of the Sweet Pea. He might have no other thought or interest in the world, such long, absorbed hours does he spend among the plants. Only a very few years ago, as it seems, he was a heedless youngster rollicking on the grass, gravely watched by his strong-jawed, close-shaven father, an actor of not inconsiderable parts, who gave him a free run. I really do not know what is going to become of the boy—nothing bad, of course, for nothing bad ever came out of flowers—but I do not believe that he will ever learn a part, or master a brief, or compose an oratorio.

You can grow very good Sweet Peas on fences, if you provide the plants with something to cling to. String is permissible, and so is galvanised wire, but I think perhaps it is best to set a row of ordinary Pea sticks against the fence and let the plants ramble on them.

I should do the same if I wanted to cover a wall with Peas sown or planted out, but the finest plants that I ever saw on walls were growing in large pots in the beautiful garden at Aldersey Hall, near Chester, where many fine varieties were raised. The pots stood near the wall. The plants were supported in them by long bamboo canes, and these, sloping till they touched the wall, linked up pot and wall. The plants were ten and eleven feet high, and they made a glorious picture. The wall—an old kitchen-garden wall of lofty stature and solid structure, grey and mellow with age—was covered with broad green leaves and brilliant blossoms. With this plan as an example, what wall can be left bare?

Have you courage to use trellis-work in your garden, reader? The "rather suburban, isn't it?" of the country gardener may not crush you, for you may be a suburbanist yourself. After all, does anyone know what "rather suburban" means, horticulturally? We know what a lady means when she says it of another lady, with a slight shrug, and an indulgent expression, "Not exactly bad form, dear, but just a little suburban." But we do not know what it means in the gardening sense, and we do not want to be told.

A suburban gardener, with a low wall or fence, or with an open side to his semi-detached house, or with an ugly object in some neighbouring garden (which really deserves to be called a yard), may turn to expanding trellis with confidence.

It has more than once served my purpose to use trellis work temporarily in a country garden, and I have never hesitated to do it. More, I have covered the stop-gap with Sweet Peas, and had a lovely display. Sweet Peas on trellis work need no wire, no sticks, no string. Their tendrils lay tight hold of the narrow slats, and cling to them with a close and entwining affection.

"Rather suburban," quotha! Give me more suburbanism if I can buy it at this price. I am sorry if it makes some of my friends feel hurt and pained, but if they like they can look the other way. And if they are driven to utter a reproachful sigh at the thought of my shamelessness—well, they must console themselves with the reflection that I am still young enough to learn the unwritten laws of gardening rectitude.

CHAPTER VIII.

OF THE SWEET PEA AS AN EXHIBITION FLOWER.

    Come paint up your boxes, the season's begun;
    There are prizes to gain, there are cups to be won,
    And win them or lose them you'll never repent
    The tussles you've had in the snowy white tent.
    In jest and in laughter old foemen unite,
    Like sportsmen they talk and like sportsmen they fight;
    Each feels that it's nothing but triumph deferred
    When he's sure that he's first, but the judge puts him
        third!

EVERYONE of us loves a flower show, in whatever capacity he goes to it. Its main features may be the same year after year, but it never grows stale. Old show-goers will tell you that they know every exhibitor's flowers by his style, and that they look for certain big plants at some of the shows as they look for the morning milk. But they go on visiting the exhibition until " clear the tents " is called for the last time, and they go out into the unknown.

A flower show is full of pleasant sights.

It is pleasant to see how full of delightful self-importance a rosette or a bit of coloured ribbon in his buttonhole will fill a committeeman. He positively distends with harmless pleasure, and we are not such contemptible curmudgeons as to refuse to share his gratification with him.

It is pleasant to see to what heights of rapture a second prize of the value of three shillings and sixpence will lift a prosperous lawyer or merchant. He chuckles gleefully as he imparts the joyful news to us. " Second, my boy, and only the third time I've competed! " We beam with him as we pour out our congratulations.

It is pleasant to observe the distant dignity of the judges before the show, and the delightful way in which they unbend when their duties are over. They stand together in a group while they are waiting to be called in—cold, reserved, un-approachable. Not one of them but knows his responsibilities too well to be seen speaking to an exhibitor until the last award has been made. Shall he be the cause of doubt creeping into the minds of other competitors? No, not a vestige of suspicion as to his impartiality shall arise. Rather than this he will cut his dearest friend dead up to the luncheon hour.

It is pleasant to see the ironical satisfaction of the cantankerous competitor. Of course! Didn't he tell you? Fourth, and anybody could see that he was an easy first. Lodge a protest? Oh no, he'd done that before, and spoke pretty straight—too straight for the committee or the judges either. He didn't say they remembered it, but there you were. You saw what had happened this time. It was just what he had expected. He didn't say that he wouldn't show again either. Most people in his place wouldn't, but if they (he flung a glance over to the tent where the committee and judges were lunching) thought they were going to frighten him out of the Society they were mistaken. We speedily perceive that the cantankerous competitor is enjoying himself to his heart's content, and waste no sympathy on him; it would spoil his pleasure if we did.

A flower show is delightful, not only because it is full of cheerful sights and sweet smells, but because it is so deliciously human. So high are our spirits that we can hardly feel as indignant as we ought when a whisper goes round that one of Bob Skittle's pair of Vegetable Marrows was really grown by Joe Pickles, and that six of the Scarlet Runners on Joe's plate were gathered from Bob's row.

As specialists in Sweet Peas we naturally feel that the classes for our favourite flower are the most interesting in the show. In what other section can be found such brilliance, such grace, such perfume? How lightsome are the stems! How beautiful are the blossoms! Loosely disposed in tall, slender vases, the Sweet Peas form an enchanting picture. We smile pityingly when we see the Carnation man sticking paper collars round the necks of his flowers, and the Rosarian striving unavailingly to relieve the flatness of his dumpy boards. They do their best, poor fellows, but strive as they may they cannot equal us.

Show committees are alive to the attraction of the Sweet Pea, and we see classes provided in every schedule, while at the largest shows there is a special Sweet Pea tent. One must be early if one wants to get round this without being squeezed and elbowed into an aching and perspiring mass. Everybody wants to get into the tent all at once, and having got there to go round opposite ways.

When a Sweet Pea enthusiast gets into a tent or hall of Sweet Peas he forgets everything else. The collar which he chose with such care in the morning may go as limp as a rag under the influence of the heat, and he will be none the wiser. The hour for lunch comes and goes, he is still busy making notes. He takes the display in mass and in detail. He glories in the enchanting vision of the long stands of flowers, he rejoices in the splendid quality of one particular variety.

It was well that a Society was formed at the first symptom of the Sweet Pea fever, for it brought Committees of experts to bear on many important matters. Rules for exhibiting were drafted, and suggestions were made for the guidance of exhibitors and judges alike. As a result we do not see Sweet Pea vases with a thick mass of flowers, or Sweet Peas associated with alien foliage. The Society does not say that any exact number of stems should be shown in each vase, but suggests twenty as a suitable number. Why not an exact number, you will ask, and so put exhibitors on exactly the same footing? Because then the judges would have to expend valuable time in counting, in order to see that the specified number was adhered to. If the judges refused this duty, on the ground that they were there to consider the quality of the flowers, and not to waste time in the schoolboy reiteration of the multiplication table, competitors would put in more or less than the number stipulated, and then there would be trouble.

It may be contended that if a competitor is not restricted to twenty stems he is sure to put in a great many more. Oh, no! he is not, for if he does he will crowd his vase, and "crowding is a defect." If he should go to the other extreme, and only put in say a dozen in order to concentrate on a few very fine stems, his vase will be ill-furnished, and the judge will have no difficulty in reckoning up the situation.

It is a totally different thing for a judge to count a stand of twenty-four varieties of Roses and a stand of twenty-four sorts of Sweet Peas, for most Rose stands are made up of single examples of each variety, whereas Sweet Pea stands contain many stems of each variety. Keep as near to twenty stems as you can, exhibitors, then you will have a vase that is neither bare nor crowded, and you will run no risk of disqualification unless, indeed, you put in eleven varieties where there should be twelve, making up two vases of one variety by some unlucky oversight.

There is one pitfall easily fallen into. Many varieties of Sweet Pea are going about under several names. What would happen if an exhibitor, acting in ignorance, put in the same variety under two names? I am very much afraid that he would be disqualified. If we break the law of the land, and are found out, it avails us nothing to declare our ignorance. The laws of the country are published, and if we do not read them we must take the consequences. The National Sweet Pea Society publishes the names of Sweet Peas, and gives duplicate names where such exist. If we do not read the Society's lists, and come to grief, we have only ourselves to blame.

The elimination of the number test makes quality decisive, and so, I aver, it ought to be. But what is quality in a Sweet Pea? Let us consider the points:

One is length of stem. When the plants are well-grown the stems will be fifteen to eighteen inches long, and if flowers are shown on stems only eight inches long the assumption is that the culture is defective. (A word to the young judge here: see that a wily exhibitor has not lengthened his stems with fine wire.)

Then there should be three to four flowers on each stem, preferably four, because when good varieties of Sweet Peas are well grown they commonly bear fours. This seems to bring in counting again, but the judge can see at a glance if there is a preponderance of twos and threes rather than of threes and fours in each vase. The flowers should be large, but they should not be spread-eagled over a considerable length of stem, and facing different ways. They should form a neat, uncrowded cluster, looking the judge in the face.

We must also consider whether a variety is in "good colour." Each has its true colour, and the judge knows it. If it is pale, or washy, or streaky, it is "out of character." If the flowers are old the colours will be dull instead of bright, and that is unpardonable. The cantankerous competitor sometimes points to his long stems, and fours, which are obvious to the most casual beholder, but he does not point to dullness, which is less obvious. In quite old flowers the keel will be open.

These are a few of the details, but the general effect is worth considering, as in a close competition it often carries the award. The colours ought to be well contrasted. It is bad policy to put a rose close to a pink, or an orange next to a salmon. The longest-stemmed varieties should go at the back. Very little foliage will be required, and no alien leafage should ever be introduced. A little Sweet Pea foliage may improve a vase, and so may a few flower sprays of *Gypsophila paniculata*, but generally nothing at all is required. Good flowers, lightly arranged and well contrasted, will suffice to satisfy the judge. Some heather or moss may be put in the mouth of the vases to keep the stems in position. It is desirable that flower stems alone be shown, not parts of the haulm also.

Many a challenge cup has been won in the garden, and lost on the way to the show. The young exhibitor thinks that his flowers are likely to suffer from dryness on their journey, and so he gathers them damp, and puts the stems in water, or wraps wet moss round them. Experience will teach him better. Wet flowers are liable to become spotted. See the old show hand at work. He cuts his flowers in blazing sunshine at noon the day before the show, when they are perfectly dry, puts the stems in water, and places the vases in a shed protected from the sun. The judging is twenty-four hours off, but there the flowers are. They are young, and they do not look very convincing; there seems to be no size, no substance, no weight about them. Well, just wait a little while. The station is three or four miles off and so a cart is got out late in the afternoon, the bunches of flowers are taken out of the water, rolled in tissue paper, with a twist of oiled or damp paper round the base of the stems, and packed firmly in ventilated boxes. The cart is loaded, and the old show hand jogs off, peacefully hopeful. Directly he gets to the show he takes out his flowers and places them in water. If he has made many entries he probably works through the night arranging his vases, has a quiet sleep beneath the stage in the small hours, and when daylight comes, proceeds to put the finishing touches on. He is not hurried, he is not flurried. He has broken the back of his task, and he has plenty of time to finish it off to his complete satisfaction. His flowers seem to have grown bigger in the night. You could be certain that they are not the same that you saw the day before. What virginal freshness is upon them too! They literally glisten. They are as fresh as a young girl just dressed after her morning bath.

Rain just before a show is not a friend to the grower, we see. It is sunshine that he wants. Perhaps a few of the varieties will have to be shaded, but only the salmon and orange-coloured flowers are likely to need it, for the florists have made the scarlets and crimsons sunproof by selecting types with thick petals. A yard or two of tiffany, which is a fine canvas that seedsmen sell, tacked on to a frame of laths and fixed above the doubtful flowers, will cost but little, and do all that is needed.

What more do we want to win silver cups with Sweet Peas? Why, a few tall rows or clumps, growing in trenched, manured, moist soil to supply the blooms. Previous chapters tell of generous soil preparation, thin planting, staking, and other details of culture. If the exhibitor means to win prizes early and late in the season he may nip off the top of every other plant at four feet high, and let the others go on to six feet before heading them. This will give him a succession of flowering growths for many weeks, and if they are kept uncrowded they are certain to produce fine flowers. If his plants are blooming profusely some time before the show, he will do well to strip them of their blooms about ten days before the exhibition, and so make sure of a supply of young flowers.

Good culture then, is the bedrock of exhibiting. We do not win the cup on the summer day that we set up our flowers in the tent, but on the winter day that we start out with the spade.

Vases are supplied at most shows where Sweet Peas are made a feature, a small charge being made for their hire. But the old show hand is likely to have his own, because he knows just how to get the effect that he wants with them. The "Jones" vase (Fig. 10), is an excellent one. It is a tall, slender, tapering glass tube, resting in a detachable metal base, to which is soldered a small plate for the name card.

Fig. 10.—JONES'S EXHIBITION OR TABLE VASE FOR SWEET PEAS.

With a little practice at home an effective, six, twelve or twenty-four can be arranged with equal ease. Some suggestions for prize stands are given in the Appendix.

CHAPTER IX.

OF THE SWEET PEA AS A MARKET FLOWER.

"Sweet Peas, who'll buy?" Hear the shrill cry!
See the thin features, mark the sad sigh!
"A bunch for a penny, sir, hunger is nigh,
Who'll buy my Sweet Peas? Sweet Peas who'll buy?"

"Sweet Peas, who'll buy?" hours swiftly fly,
Pleasure's gay suitors pass heedlessly by,
Piteous the pleading voice, weary the eye,
"Who'll buy my Sweet Peas? Sweet Peas, who'll buy?"

"Sweet Peas, who'll buy?" Hear the reply
Of children in garrets who sicken and die:
"Buy mother's bunches, sir, starving we lie.
Who'll buy her Sweet Peas? Sweet Peas, who'll buy?"

"Sweet Peas, who'll buy?" Voices on high
Ask us to listen and bid us comply:
"We sit here together, our sister and I
Who'll buy our Sweet Peas? Come, hasten and buy."

FOR those of us who have abundant garden space in which to grow Sweet Peas the bunches of flowers in the windows of small town houses have a touch of pathos, still more have those which we catch sight of in the open windows of the hospitals. An impulse of pity leaps up within us. Our minds had been so full of the charm of our flowers, we had grown so absorbed in the delights of our garden, we had become so preoccupied with the interest of our seedlings, that we had almost forgotten that there was an outside world at all, much less a host of shadowed lives, pursuing their sad and painful round in gloomy town buildings.

The sight of the flowers reminds us at once of the existence of these people and of their kinship with us. They love beauty and fragrance just as we do, and they need flowers more. In happier circumstances they would not be working in a dull factory, or wearily counting the flies on the walls of a sick ward; they would be gloating over their new salmon Spencer, which has flowers of the size of a watch face, and never burns even in the fiercest sunshine.

The bunches in the windows have a certain similarity, the colours are the same, and the method of arrangement (which invariably consists in packing the flowers in one solid mass) is similar. The only difference is in the receptacle which holds them. It is often a pickle bottle, but sometimes it is a jug without a handle, and occasionally it is a jam jar. There is no irritating affectation of Art here. There is nothing pretentious or artificial. It is good, honest, elementary crudity. There is the jug which carried the family beer during its early days, there are the flowers, and in they go. But the great thing is that flower love is stirring. Who knows but that, in special family conclave, beer has been given up to admit flowers? Has it escaped attention that a fall in the dividends of breweries has coincided with the rise of Sweet Peas?

Townsfolk of all classes love Sweet Peas. They delight in the brilliant colours of the flowers, they enjoy the delicious perfume. They would grow Sweet Peas if they could, and as they cannot grow them they buy them. Here is the market grower's opportunity. But let not the youngster who is just leaving a horticultural college, and is looking for an opening as a market gardener, jump eagerly to the conclusion that the Sweet Pea mine is quite unworked, and full of rich ore. Although the general public only took up Sweet Peas with the twentieth century, a good many people quietly loved and bought the flowers years before. They were townsfolk of the well-to-do class, who did not mind paying a good price. The owner of the handleless jug has but a few coppers to spare for flowers, and he wants a lot for his money. More flowers are bought than ever there were, but prices are low, and market growers must not expect to make large fortunes out of Sweet Peas nowadays.

Town buyers are very particular as to colours. They do not want many. They adore pink, they love white, they like lavender, they appreciate salmon. The favourite pink of the London market is Countess Spencer, the favourite white Nora Unwin (with dear old Dorothy Eckford holding her own well), the favourite lavenders Frank Dolby and Lady Grizel Hamilton. Helen Lewis (the orange Countess) and the old salmon pink Miss Willmott sell well. As time passes the plain standards will probably tend to decline, giving way more and more to waved sorts.

The north country markets differ a little from the southern ones. They like the deep, rich colours, such as scarlet and crimson; consequently, such varieties as Queen Alexandra, King Edward VII., John Ingman, and E. J. Castle are more profitable than the mauves and pinks. The youngster from the horticultural college, or anybody else who sets out to make money from Sweet Pea bloom, will see from this that he has to study the different markets. Why Manchester prefers John Ingman and London Countess Spencer is not clear. To ascertain the cause might mean deep psychological probing. Market growers have no time for psychology; they hasten to take facts as they are, and let the reasons look after themselves. But let it not be inferred that the southern favourites are disliked in Lancashire and Yorkshire. "Oadham" likes Countess Spencer, and "Poodsa" is very keen on Frank Dolby.

The number of sprays to the bunch depends mainly on the size and quality of the flowers. Twelve good spikes make a satisfactory bunch early in the season, but later on, when the keenness of the demand has spent itself it is advisable to give eighteen. Some growers pack their bunches so that the front of all the flowers faces the same way, thus forming a fan-shaped bunch; but the best way is to take the spikes in the hand and bump the ends lightly on the table so as to get them level, then tie the stems lightly quite low down. While this secures the stems it leaves the flowers loose. Some stems are longer than others, and so much the better, as the flowers stand up above the rest, and a lighter, looser, more graceful effect is secured. Moreover, the bunches do not heat so quickly in transit as they do when the flowers are in one mass.

Market growers find that it is wise to sow in Autumn when the soil is warm and well drained and the situation sheltered, because the bloom comes a week earlier, and is of better quality, than from spring-sown seed, and better prices are realised. But it is futile to sow in autumn on cold, damp soil, in an exposed situation. With the right soil and site the plants will stand almost any weather. True, a sharp frost after rain or melted snow may do harm, cutting them back almost to the level of the ground, but even then they are likely to break up from the base and make good plants. Moral: get the right soil and site if you want the most profits. If soil and site are not what they should be, the seed had better be sown in pots and put in cold frames about the middle of October. If the seed is to be sown out of doors, let it be put in about the end of September. One pound may be allowed to every 120 yards of drill and the rows may be five and a half feet apart. A little mound of soil may be drawn along each side of the row to protect the plants.

Much has been said about deep trenching for exhibition Sweet Peas, but the market grower cannot afford this luxury. The crop really would not pay for it, as the flowers are rarely worth picking after they have been on the market about three weeks. Now, plants on ground that has been simply well dug, and enriched with manure worked in to a depth of ten inches, at the rate of twenty-five loads per acre, will produce excellent flowers for that short period; and the process is far cheaper than trenching.

In March the sticks should be placed to the plants, and they (the sticks) should be long and strong.

The first flowers of the outdoor-sown plants ought to be ready by the end of May. Readiness is not, of course, synonymous with full expansion. The stems should always be picked while the flowers are in an early stage, with no more than two open, then they may be expected to reach the market in a fresh, attractive state. If they are gathered with all the flowers open some of them are likely to drop if the weather is warm. Flowers should never be gathered and packed while wet, or they will heat and rot. Two or three dozen bunches may be packed in a flower box, lined with white or blue paper, and no wool or moss should be used. If young and dry the flowers will travel well and open out into freshness and beauty.

The grower will very likely find it to his advantage to tap the London market for the first week and the northern markets for the remainder of the season.

With respect to the pot frame plants, it will be well to plunge the pots in cinders for protection from frost. But the plants should not be shut up and coddled all the winter; on the contrary, the frames should be kept open, except in bad weather. If the soil is in workable condition the plants may be put out about the middle of March, shaking any loose soil off carefully, and putting clumps of three or four plants together fifteen inches apart. The sticks should be put in at once, as they will help to shelter the plants. The soil may be slightly mounded. Early in May half an ounce of nitrate of soda may be sprinkled along each yard of row and very lightly pointed in, but it must be kept off the plants. These plants ought to bloom early in June.

Lastly as to the prices—the most important point of all. Once upon a time the grower could expect to start with 3s. 6d. to 4s. per dozen bunches, and finish at 1s.; the average paid him very well. Nowadays he often has to start with 2s., 1s. 6d., or even 1s.; and finish with sixpence per dozen bunches. At these prices he does not find himself in a position to retire with a competency at the end of his first year. In fact, he is fortunate if there is a margin on the right side. The management must be good to show a profit.

CHAPTER X.

OF THE SWEET PEA UNDER GLASS.

If you really love a garden you must love a greenhouse too,
Cowper said it long ago and certainly it's true.
Buy a hundred flower pots, buy a sack of loam,
And be the weather what it may you've flowers in the home.

The hundredth seedsman's sent along his Sweet Pea catalogue,
You light your pipe and on the fire you place a portly log,
You choose a score of charming sorts, a novelty or two,
And later on your wife proceeds to show what she can do.

She takes the pretty blossoms and she takes a dainty bowl;
It's winter time and angry clouds across the heavens roll,
But you see no pettish pouting, you hear no heavy sighs,
For sunshine in her heart and home illume the gloomy skies.

WHEN some friend in the country sends a flower-loving townsman a box of Sweet Peas before April is out the latter knows quite well that they have been grown under glass. "Hustle" may expedite matters outdoors to some extent but it will not give Sweet Peas before Easter. Nature is not going to be rushed and worried as a team of professional footballers rush and worry a ball into goal.

The flowers bring a great gush of sunshine with them, and cheer us up. Perhaps we are suffering from "spring slackness." A hard winter has tried us. East winds have kept both the garden and ourselves in a minor key. There is no bloom out of doors, and not a shred of spirit in ourselves. We open the box and a rush of fragrance greets our nostrils. We unfold the tissue paper, and we see exquisite blossoms of pink, scarlet, white and rose. The surprise is complete. An involuntary cry of astonishment and admiration escapes our lips. Our spirits go up with a bound. The world is born anew for us. We recall all the joys of last year's wanderings among the flowers. We are filled with happy anticipation of equal pleasure this. The east wind loses its piercing quality. The skies lose their gloom. Such is the magic influence of a handful of flowers.

If this experience has been yours, reader, as it has been mine, you may, perhaps, have followed my example, and hastened to the fountain head, not wholly for the purpose of proffering your thanks in person, but partly to learn how the thing is done. Such length of stem, such size of bloom, such richness of colour, all produced nearly three months before the usual flowering season, must, you tell yourself, indicate a remarkable system of culture. So you send off a hasty postcard, consult a time-table, and the next day the smiling magician meets you at a country station, delighted to lead you to his greenhouses, and show all that there is to see.

What a vision of beauty is there! You enter a long span-roof house, hardly knowing what you expect to see, but with a general thought of orthodox plants in orthodox pots on an orthodox stage. Instead, you see a long row of plants growing in a trench cut along the centre of the path, the stems supported by a framework of bamboo canes and wire carried to the ridge. The plants are trained scientifically. Planted thirty inches apart, their shoots are arranged and tied almost like the branches of a fan shaped Peach tree. There is no crossing, no crowding. All is order. The stems are nearly flat, and more than half an inch broad. The flower stalks are fifteen to eighteen inches long, and the blossoms are of great size and splendid colour.

The plants are growing in large pots, but when the trench was made some loam and manure were put at the bottom, and roots have hastened out of the pot to feed on them.

Nothing impresses you more than the strong side growths of the plants. They have broken out from near the base. Some of them have been stopped by picking off the tip and have pushed sublaterals, strong, and bearers of magnificent flowers.

Well, clearly we cannot all grow Sweet Peas in this way. We do not possess wide, lofty span-roof greenhouses, in the path of which we can make trenches. Perhaps, though, we have a fairly spacious conservatory, and if so we may, if we will, choose Sweet Peas as one of the plants with which to decorate it. If we want spring bloom we must sow in autumn, thinly in small pots, but we need not give heat until the New Year. The plants will be all right in a frame till then. We can transfer them from small pots to medium, and then from medium to large—say 4-inch to 6-inch, and 6 inch to 8 or 9-inch by successive stages, giving the shift when the smaller pots are full of roots. If we do not want early bloom it will suffice to sow in February. In both cases the soil may consist of loam, with a quarter part of leaf-mould or decayed manure and some sand. We must guard carefully against crowding of the growths. If side shoots come too abundantly some must be pinched out (Fig. 11). Six growths in all, whether from one plant or more, will suffice for each pot. They must

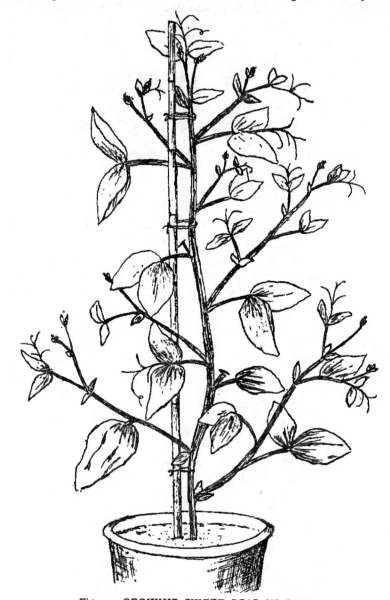

Fig 11.—GROWING SWEET PEAS IN POTS.
Note some of the side shoots removed at the bars to prevent crowding.
The strong side shoots left will all flower well.

be tied securely to tall, strong stakes, such as bamboo, well embedded in the soil. With a thicker mass of growth it might be preferable to use well-trimmed Pea sticks.

The plants are not likely to be attacked by insects, but the house may be vaporised with one of the advertised cones every fortnight, for the protection of other plants. The ventilators should be opened in fine weather in order to maintain a free circulation of air. There must be regular watering, and a weekly dose of liquid manure may be given when the plants come into bloom. A light dewing over through a syringe will be highly beneficial on the evening of sunny days.

All the flowers should be gathered young, then there will be no running to seed with its attendant exhaustion.

The grower may, if he likes, transfer some of the strongest of his plants in their large pots (or in tubs, if he should use these in preference to pots), to selected positions in the garden when they come into bloom; either because they have grown too bulky for the conservatory, or because there are a few special places opposite the windows where the plants would be likely to show to advantage. The ability to make such provision is an added reason for growing a few Sweet Peas in pots.

Most of the popular garden Sweet Peas, such as Countess Spencer, Helen Lewis, Nora Unwin, Frank Dolby, Lady Grizel Hamilton, Dorothy Eckford and King Edward VII., are suitable for growing in pots.

But if the grower wants bloom at midwinter he must get seed of a special strain, which the large seedsmen offer.

These, also the Telemly Sweet Peas developed in Algiers by the Rev. E. Arkwright, and the strain selected by Mr. C. Engelmann, of Saffron Walden, will bloom at Christmas if sown in September. They are charming flowers—all Sweet Peas are charming—but it is idle to pretend that they are more than a shadow of the modern garden types.

Mont Blanc is a very early blooming white Sweet Pea, and it is of dwarf growth, so that it is suitable for pot culture.

Let me stop here. I would gladly go on to say that our beautiful favourite is well adapted for every amateur's greenhouse in the land if I could do so conscientiously, but I cannot. Some of those little glass boxes that we know of give a wonderful amount of enjoyment to the sturdy, flower-loving artizans who own them, but I cannot very well say that they are adapted for Sweet Peas, except so far as concerns the raising of seedlings. A collection of Zonal Geraniums, if you like—yes, and good Geraniums too, with fine, big, round flowers in large, handsome trusses—a few pots of tuberous Begonias, even a Cucumber, planted in a mound on the stage and trained under the roof, but Sweet Peas—no.

The best of things has its limitations, and we must sorrow fully admit that the Sweet Pea as a pot plant is hardly suitab for the list of our friend Jack Smitham, of 747, Foundry Stree Steelville. Jack is a terrible fellow for flowers, and whe the prizes are given away after the annual show of the Stee ville Horticultural Society he is trotting backwards an forwards all the time, looking shiningly clean after his week shave. He grows an astonishing number of things in th glass box of his, in fact, how he packs them in without squeezir all the beauty out of them is a secret known only to himsel but with all his gifts of compression he cannot manage collection of Sweet Peas in pots. He grows his Sweet Peas clumps along the side of his allotment, and if you noticed the prize-giving, he took first prize for them.

CHAPTER XI.

ON THE ENEMIES OF THE SWEET PEA.

> With the slug and the grub and the worm,
> With the root-rot, the mould and the streak,
> The florist might surely affirm
> That his chances of bloom are but weak.
> On the leaf and the stem there are foes,
> There's an enemy down at the roots,
> But in spite of these worries and woes
> There are beautiful flowers on the shoots.

WHEN we read of the interminable list of human diseases we wonder that we are alive. It seems impossible that we can escape them all. But somehow many of us jog along very well for seventy or eighty years, and only come to grief in the end owing to an unlucky misunderstanding with a motor-car.

When a lover of Sweet Peas realises how many enemies his plants have he is overcome by misgivings of utter disaster. If wireworm does not attack his seedlings it seems certain that slugs, or surface caterpillars, or leather jackets will. Should none of these pests annihilate the plants, mildew, or mould, or streak, or eelworm, or root-rot will. To escape every insect and fungus seems impossible. But the weeks pass, the rains fall, the plants grow, the flowers open. Before we fully realise it the season has come and gone, and the only enemy that proves to have any power over the plants is Old Father Time himself. He is the one triumphant, unconquerable foe. We can dress, dust, and spray; we can concoct insecticides and fungicides; but in the end the scythe sweeps round and our plants fall. Old Time has an impervious skin, which sprays cannot penetrate. His internal mechanism is such that he can feast gaily on poisons. Nor lime, nor Vaporite, nor Bordeaux mixture, nor soot, nor lead arsenate, can disturb his anatomy.

Pessimists are not wanting who prophesy that sooner or later some virulent Sweet Pea disease—some special enemy provided by outraged Nature—must come to punish us for giving our plants unnatural treatment. "Look at the

Hollyhock," they may say; "look at the Potato; look at the Carnation!" Well, of course, all of these plants are harassed by injurious fungi, but in spite of them we get Hollyhocks, we get Potatoes, and we get Carnations. The chances for Sweet Peas are greater rather than less, because the system of propagation adopted is the natural one—that of seeds.

It is not clear that we need expect a special Sweet Pea disease. We do not practise intensive vegetative systems of increase—that act which of all others gives the greatest predisposition to disease. We do not coddle the plants in a hot, close atmosphere. We do, it is true, interfere with Nature to the extent of deferring the seeding by cutting off the flowers while young, but that tends to keep the plants healthy rather than to bring about disease. The whole course of culture is in the direction of strengthening and fortifying the plants. By giving them the best of soil, plenty of room and adequate support, we give them a better chance of vigorous, healthy growth than they would have in a state of Nature.

We hear more about the attacks of insects and fungi on Sweet Peas than we used to do, but this is due to the fact that so many more Sweet Peas are grown than in former days. There are more diseased plants because there are so many more plants. There are more complaints because there are so many more growers to complain. In the days when Sweet Peas were only grown in a few gardens, and were taken little notice of, it is not to be expected that so much would be heard of enemies as is the case now that Sweet Peas are grown in every garden, and are made the subject of minute and careful study.

Let us flatly refuse to be oppressed by gloomy forebodings of impending disaster. Let us practise a gay and cheerful optimism. As for our culture being unnatural—tush! It is unnatural to scrub ourselves with soap of a morning, but science and practical experience both teach us that we are the better for the scrubbing. The more care we take of our young Sweet Peas (care, be it understood, being quite distinct from coddling), and the stronger we grow them, the more likely disease is to keep away. The worst enemy of Sweet Peas is not the slug, nor the wireworm, nor the leather-jacket, nor the mildew, nor the streak, but the man who grows his plants thickly in poor soil and never gives them any attention.

Let us see the worst that certain pests can do to Sweet Peas, and the worst that we can do to the pests.

THE ENEMIES OF THE SWEET PEA.

Wireworm.—It is well known that freshly-broken pasture land is liable to be infested with wireworm, because the roots of grass afford it sustenance. Lucky the gardener who, having turned a meadow into a garden, does not find himself involved in a long fight with wireworm. If he takes the turf away and stacks it, so that it may rot down into potting soil, he takes away most of the wireworm with it (see chapter V.), and although some are always left behind, yet the battle is more than half won. If he turns the turf down so as to get the benefit of its rich store of nitrates he preserves the wireworm with it. What is your choice, reader? But you want to hear my opinion. It is to read my opinions that you have bought my book. Let me give it to you with an all-embracing emphasis—an emphasis that brooks no qualification and no reservation, which has neither doubt nor hesitation. Do *not* turn in undecayed turf. If you like to take it away, stack it until it has rotted, and replace it; or if you like to remove it, char it and replace it, well and good. In either case the worst that can be said of you is that in your earnestness you have given yourself a good deal of hard work. Of the intrinsic merits of either plan there can be no doubt. Do either, but do not turn the turf in untreated. You may put it two feet down if you like, but the wireworm will not stay there with it. He will come up ravenous. Sowing ground with Mustard and turning it in green, and dressing with Vaporite or Apterite, are approved methods of reducing wireworm. Special plants may be protected by inserting baits of Carrot or Potato near them.

Slugs.—The slug is very destructive in some seasons, and harmless in others. The Sweet Pea has no special attraction for him, but if he is present in numbers which put a severe strain on the food supply, he will attack Sweet Peas. When he starts he often carries things to a point which leaves the grower in despair. Raisers of new varieties have assured me that the slug has a maddening aptitude for finding out and devouring their choicest seedlings. When there are novelties about, commoners have no charm for him. Freshly slaked lime is a potent safeguard against slugs. It is best used in two forms: as a powder sprinkled along the rows beside the plants, and renewed after rain; and as lime water distributed over the garden through a rosed can at night. To get the powder, sprinkle some lumps of lime fresh from the kiln with a little water, and they will crumble down with emission of heat. To make the lime water, put a lump of lime as large as a cocoanut in a pail of water, and let it stand for a few hours. As an additional precaution heaps of brewers' grains may be put near the most valuable plants as a bait, and examined at night, when any slugs which are found can be destroyed instantaneously by dropping them in a vessel of salt and water.

Weevil.—Perhaps the reader has seen neat notches cut in the leaves of his Sweet Peas in the spring, and has wondered which one of Nature's tailors has been at work with sharp and well-trained scissors. It is the weevil known as *Sitones lineatus*, and as, in addition to its attack on the foliage, its larva feeds on the roots, it is capable of working great mischief. Perhaps the slug sometimes gets the credit of some of the injury which this enemy does, anyway, those who notice young plants going off in spring would do well to make a careful investigation before they put the damage down to their old enemy. Even a slug deserves justice. The weevil is about a quarter of an inch long, dark on the upper side, with grey lines, clayey beneath, and therefore difficult to distinguish when it has dropped from the plants on to its back and lies motionless, which it does promptly if disturbed. The best way to stamp out an attack is to reduce the soil to a fine tilth, keep it close and firm, dust lime along the rows, and in extreme cases spray a mixture of paraffin and soft soap at the rate of half-a-pint of the former and one pint of the latter to five gallons of water (first boiling the soft soap) over the plants.

Mould or Blight.—If the lower leaflets of young Sweet Pea plants become affected with small yellow patches in early summer, which spread and eventually cause the leaves to shrivel; and if the trouble extends upwards, the presence of Pea mould (*Peronospora trifoliorum var. viciæ*) may be suspected. The patches may be covered with a grey mould and the roots shrivel. The plants should be dusted with powdered quicklime and sulphur, two parts of the former and one part of the latter, directly the disease is noticed. The powder is best applied with a Malbec bellows while the leaves are damp, especially on the under side. Or they may be sprayed with a solution of liver of sulphur (sulphide of potassium) half an ounce per gallon of water. The following fertiliser may be pointed in near the plants at the rate of one ounce per yard : superphosphate 1 part, kainit 1 part, nitrate of soda ½ part, sulphate of iron ½ part. All diseased growths should be burned, and the crop should be put on fresh ground the following year. The disease is worst in wet, cold seasons.

Spot.—The leaves of Sweet Peas sometimes become marked by small, whity-brown or greenish spots, which generally lie below the surface of the leaf, and in some cases fall out, leaving small holes. This disease is known as spot (*Ascochyta pisi*). It may be checked by spraying with Bordeaux mixture, which can be made as follows:—(1) dissolve ½-lb. bluestone (sulphate of copper) in a wooden vessel containing a little water, (2) put ½-lb. of quicklime in a gallon of water and let the vessel stand a few hours, (3) pour the two liquids together in a tub containing enough water to bring the total quantity up to five gallons. Badly affected plants should be burned.

Root-rot.—Sweet Peas sometimes grow strongly up to a certain stage, then yellow veins appear on the leaves, the tops of the plants become stunted and turn over, and they die. This may happen when they are only a foot high, or when they have nearly reached the flowering stage. It is the root-rot disease (*Thielavia basicola*). If it should appear, the plant should be supported by pointing in half-an-ounce each of sulphate of potash and sulphate of iron along each yard run of row. Badly affected plants should be burned. In preparing fresh ground plenty of wood ashes should be dug in, and basic slag and kainit may be applied at the rate of seven pounds of each per square rod in autumn.

Mildew.—The greyish mould which sometimes spreads over the plants is the fungus *Erysiphe polygoni*. It is rarely troublesome when the plants are well grown, but it often affects weak plants badly. Good soil should be provided, and growth may be stimulated with liquid manure. At the same time an effort may be made to destroy the first patches of mildew by making one of the applications advised under mould.

Streak.—Plants with grey lines on the leaves, and with flabby, streaky flowers, are sometimes seen. The conjunction of the two caused growers to suspect a new disease, to which the name "streak" was applied. Serious misgivings were entertained respecting it. A number of plants which I had on freshly broken pasture in 1907 were badly affected in this way. I do not think that streak is a new disease, and I think it likely that there is no connection between the affection of the leaves and that of the flowers. The appearance of the leaves is probably due to an attack of one of the fungi already named, or to root worms (see below), and that of the flowers to green fly (see below).

Green Fly.—This well-known green aphis sometimes attacks the foliage of Sweet Peas, although it is not generally a serious pest, and it may be kept under by dusting with tobacco powder and afterwards syringing vigorously. But I think that it often affects flowers in a manner not suspected. Establishing itself on the buds it sucks the juices and causes the colours to "run," so that the flowers look muddled and streaky. More than once a grower has seized on one of these variations as a new break.

Root Worms.—Root worms are of two kinds, the eelworm and the white-worm. The presence of one or other may be suspected if a young plant suddenly becomes stunted and shortly afterwards collapses completely, the stems withering and the roots rotting. Such plants should be burnt, together with the soil near them. The growth of the others should be stimulated with liquid manure. A splendid chemical fertiliser is nitrate of potash, an ounce of which may be dissolved in a gallon of water, and applied every other day for a week.

Birds.—Aggrieved amateurs speak of injury from birds at two stages : when the seeds are freshly sown, and when the plants are in bud. Birds are certainly fond of Pea seeds, and while I think that they are more partial to culinary than to Sweet Peas, I approve of the simple precaution of moistening the seeds with paraffin or linseed oil, and then rolling them in red lead before sowing. Paraffin alone suffices as a rule, but in some places the bird pest is present in special force. Complaints of young birds pecking off Sweet Pea buds are more common in dry than in wet seasons. No doubt bird lovers will tell us that the birds are less concerned to prevent us winning a particular Challenge Cup than to find moisture for themselves, but whatever their object the result is the same. Syringing with soot water, or the use of scares, may be suggested as preventives.

Mice.—The field mouse, ever ready to change his quarters and become a garden mouse, has always had a weakness for Peas. He loves them when they are swollen and tender with the juices of germination. Many a time and oft he has got the seedsman (who, on the strength of a 100 per cent. growth in his trial book, glows with indignation at any reflection on the germinating power of his seeds) a "wigging" from an impulsive amateur. Really, if Peas do not come up it is not always the fault of the seedsman. The oil and red lead device mentioned in the paragraph on birds discourages mice also. Small traps, baited with Peas or cheese, may be set as an additional precaution.

Caterpillars.—As one of the photographs shows, Sweet Peas are sometimes attacked by caterpillars. They should be picked off and destroyed.

CHAPTER XII.

OF THE VARIETIES OF SWEET PEAS.

Scarlet are the Sweet Peas, the Sweet Peas, the Sweet Peas,
Scarlet are the Sweet Peas, that dance the hours away;
There's many a dainty colour in the fragrant little Heartsease,
But it has no coat that exactly suits the red of a hunting day.

Shining blue are the Sweet Peas, the Sweet Peas, the Sweet Peas,
Shining blue are the Sweet Peas that cling to the hazel spray,
There's many a sky tint borrowed by the heaving waves of the deep seas,
But it isn't the hue of the bluetit's coat as he twitters his little lay.

White as snow are the Sweet Peas, the Sweet Peas, the Sweet Peas,
White as snow are the Sweet Peas, so lightsome in their play,
There's white in many a fragrant Stock that brings the hum of the big bees,
But it isn't the white of the Hawthorn bloom in the merry month of May.

THE student of Sweet Peas loses himself in a maze of colour variations, but it is a maze so delightful that he never wishes to extricate himself from it. He is content to wander on from year to year, sometimes a little dazed, always more than a little bewildered, never so absolutely sure of himself as to undertake willingly the task of naming a collection of flowers for the amateur who has mixed up his labels.

Up to a point it is fairly easy to group the Sweet Pea colours. We might work from white to crimson with the white ground flowers in the following stages :—
 (1) Etta Dyke, white.
 (2) Lady Althorp, white with a faint suffusion of pink.
 (3) Elsie Herbert, white with pink edge.
 (4) Mrs. Hardcastle Sykes, blush.
 (5) Countess Spencer, pink.
 (6) Olive Ruffell, rose.
 (7) John Ingman, carmine rose.
 (8) Sunproof Crimson, or Mrs. Duncan, crimson.
Thus we get to a deep self flower in eight easy stages.

With the yellow grounds we might proceed as follows :—
(1) Clara Curtis, cream.
(2) Evelyn Hemus, or Mrs. C. W. Breadmore, cream with pink edge.
(3) Gladys Burt, Mrs. Hugh Dickson, or Mrs. Henry Bell, cream with pink border.
(4) Constance Oliver, pink with cream centre.

And so again reach the selfs.

Or we might work up to scarlet by :—
(1) Clara Curtis, cream.
(2) Audrey Crier, pink with salmon suffusion.
(3) Earl Spencer, salmon.
(4) George Stark, scarlet.

The stages of the blue shades might be :—
(1) Mrs. Higginson, Jun., Lady Grizel Hamilton, or True Lavender, lavender.
(2) Masterpiece, lavender with rose suffusion.
(3) Flora Norton Spencer or Zephyr, medium blue.
(4) Asta Ohn, lilac.
(5) Lord Nelson, deep blue.
(6) Horace Wright, violet blue.
(7) The Marquis, mauve.
(8) Menie Christie, magenta.

These gradations are not difficult to follow, but fortunately or unfortunately the florist will not leave the matter there. He shows us whole strings of sorts which come very close to one or other of those in our lists, and he assures us that they are true. We meet him at a show, and he has a cream with a pink edge in his buttonhole. We wish to be pleasing and polite, and we say: "Ah, Mrs. Henry Bell, and very nicely grown, too." A change comes over his features. He looks half pained, half disgusted. We feel that we have "put our foot in it." However, he recovers himself, and even assumes a pitying expression as he asks: "When did you ever see Mrs. Henry Bell with as rich a colour on the edge as this?" Here he extracts Mrs. Henry Bell from a convenient box, and places it alongside of the flower in his buttonhole, "What do you say now?"

What can we say? We can see a difference between the flowers, and we hasten to say so—perhaps with a little extra emphasis because of having unwittingly ruffled him.

We go from grower to grower, and each shows us selections on his grounds that differ in a greater or less degree (it is always in a greater degree according to the grower himself) from the standard colours. There really is a difference on the particular soil, and in the particular climate, of the particular grower; yet when we transfer them to our own gardens we sometimes have to rub our eyes very wide open to enable ourselves to see it, and if the varieties were mixed up in a box we could not separate them.

In such circumstances what are we to do? Those of us who have time, and ground and money enough can grow them all, and make our own comparisons; we become, in a word, specialists. The situation has its charms. We may be asked to judge at a show, we may have long letters (the stamping of which was inadvertently overlooked) sent to us from anxious novices athirst for information. If, however, time, ground and money are scarce we cannot aspire to such distinctions as these, and thus, the arrival of the seed catalogues throws us into a terrible quandary. We do not know what to choose.

In an appendix to the present work a catalogue of varieties of Sweet Peas, together with selections, is given. That appendix will be brought up to date each time that an opportunity arises through the demand for a new edition. And the beginner has another source of information in the official lists of the National Sweet Pea Society. This most estimable institution issues two lists annually that are helpful to beginners. The first is a "Classification list," and the second a "Too much alike" list. The former gives the names of the varieties which the Society thinks are the best in their respective colours. In the latter are grouped those which are so nearly alike that they must not be exhibited in the same stand. The Society's publications, the gardening papers, and many of the Sweet Pea catalogues, contain these lists. With them to guide him the beginner need never be worried over the choice of sorts.

Let us, however, glance at a few notable Sweet Peas—varieties which are likely to live in spite of the redhot " extra special, all the winners, latest cricket scores " rush of competing novelties.

There is a Pea which bears exquisitely waved flowers, which produces four on a stem, which grows vigorously, which flowers freely, which has a colour as soft as a pink Orchid, and yet as bright as a Tulip, which is fixed, which is as beautiful a garden as it is an exhibition variety, which looks charming on a dinner table—a variety in which grace of form and beauty of colour are delightfully blended. It would be futile for me to set you the riddle of naming my Pea. You know at once that it must be the peerless, the lovely, the delicious Countess Spencer. Do you want the Countess with a gleam of gold instead of silver in her beautiful heart? You get her under the name of Constance Oliver. Both are larger, richer and better in form and waving than Gladys Unwin.

If you and I, readers, were desperadoes who had to be banished to a desert island, and were given the privilege of taking one variety of Sweet Pea with us, which would it be? (Do I see a cunning twinkle deep down in the eye of one of the criminals? It means—such is the depth of his depravity—that he would select an unfixed sort, in the hope of getting several colours to break in it, and so give him the material for selecting several varieties.) But, fixed or unfixed, it would be a pink. We might choose that tender hued Spencer, Mrs. Hardcastle Sykes—a variety of ravishing beauty, soft of hue as the clinging fingers of a babe, with flowers of huge size and perfect shape. Many Sweet Pea growers consider this to be superior even to Countess Spencer itself, and give it the palm as the most beautiful of all Sweet Peas. Differing from both, being pale pink with a shade of salmon, is the lovely Zarina.

The noble John Ingman, large of bloom, gracefully waved, and generous in its production of four per stem, of a brilliant carmine rose colour, but with more than a suspicion of deep orange in the standard, is a variety which we can hardly dispense with, whether we grow it under this name, or that of George Herbert. The rich rose, Marjorie Willis, would run John Ingman close in the race for popularity were it not for the magenta suffusion in it.

We must have a selection of orange Spencer, whether Helen Lewis, or Edrom Beauty, or Maggie Stark, or Edna Unwin, for a well selected stock has all the qualities of the true Countess Spencer type, with a rich and distinctive colour. The last is a much finer Pea than St. George.

Spencerism does not flow so freely over the scarlet as the pink Sweet Peas, and it is apt to be associated with a want of texture that results in burning, but for the matter of that the first real scarlet self—Scarlet Gem—one of the old plain standard type, was too flimsy to stand the sun. Queen Alexandra was better. George Stark has Spencer grace, vivid colour, and sufficient substance to keep its character in sunshine.

The early crimsons, both old and Spencer types, were subject to burning, but in King Edward Spencer, Mrs. Duncan and Sunproof Crimson we have varieties of brilliant colour that do not burn—large flowers and well waved withal. They have superseded the old type King Edward. The florists selected most of them out of John Ingman. They eliminated the rose, the carmine and the orange, and put crimson in its place—surely a feat of legerdemain worthy of the highest praise.

There is no patience like the patience of the florist. It carries him triumphantly through everything. Such is my faith in it that I look to be able to record in some future edition of this work, success in a task which at the time of preparing the first issue seems hopeless—that of giving vigour of growth and substance of petal to the salmon Spencers. Such of these as exist at the time of writing have the weakness for burning of the original plain standard salmon, Henry Eckford, with more constitutional flabbiness. Only the best of culture, supported by shading when the plants come into flower, can insure good blooms of Nancy Perkin and Earl Spencer. When we get the vigorous, sunproof salmon what a treasure we shall have! Societies will stumble over each other in their haste to give it awards. Seedsmen will be besieged by clamorous amateurs, scrambling for seed. (Raiser of the sunproof salmon, a word in your ear. Let us away into yonder quiet corner, lest we be overheard. Are you inexperienced in the ways of florists? Are the mysteries of the seed trade a sealed book to you? Then you want a practical adviser, one of a generous nature, who will give you the vast benefits of his knowledge for a paltry half share in the profits. A letter addressed to me will have attention. You take me? It is well.)

Pink and salmon being colours which amateurs love, what of a Sweet Pea which combines both—pink, let us say, with a suffusion of salmon? Just this, that such a variety must have as ardent a following as a pure pink, provided it comes true. There's the rub. We have a pink with suffusion of salmon; its name is Audrey Crier. But, alas! endeavours to "fix" it have hitherto proved futile. It seems incredible, but year after year passes, the most expert florists work at it, and still it throws "rogues" in exasperating profusion. Audrey Crier is the most baffling, the most perplexing, of Sweet Peas. It is adorable, but impossible. It overjoys and infuriates us by turns. An amateur comes to me and rubs his hands. "Odd, all this I hear about Audrey Crier not being fixed," he says; "it is all right with me." He is secretly exultant. He gives one the impression that he considers he has done something profoundly clever. His family all catch scarlet fever, his most important shares slump badly, but he remains cheerful: he has Audrey Crier true. The next year there is a different story to be told. His family is riotously healthy, his shares have soared again, but he is gloomy and depressed: Audrey Crier has broken up once more!

A good white Sweet Pea is as indispensable as a summer holiday. Our delight in it is so hearty and sincere that it refreshes us like the famous ozone breezes of Margate. The whites have ever been kind to us. They have been pure in hue, free in bloom, early and true. We have always loved the whites. We loved dear old Mont Blanc and Mrs. Sankey, and Blanche Burpee, and Queen of England, and Sadie Burpee and Dorothy Eckford and other old type whites. We love the modern waved varieties, like Nora Unwin and Etta Dyke. These snowy Spencers have an irresistible charm, with their exquisitely curved and pure flowers. They are delightful in the garden, winning on the table, pleasing on the show stand. A woman can overcome us by arranging a few white Sweet Peas as completely as she can by fingering, with downcast eyes, a tiny laced pocket-handkerchief. They were provided for the sex by a special dispensation of Providence.

I am as hopeful about the yellow Sweet Pea as about the sunproof salmon, and I expect to issue a special edition in its honour before my first is many years old. When we get more than a cream and only a little less than a primrose, when we see a clear canary coloured band on the edge of one flower and a gleam of gold in the centre of another, have we not food for hope? But "all is not gold that glitters." A waggish florist has shown me a Buttercup yellow Sweet Pea before now, and has gone off chuckling gleefully when I have returned it with the laconic admonishment "Get out." Anyone can make a cream Sweet Pea yellow by subjecting it to the fumes of ammonia, and no law has yet been passed by a lagging legislature for the summary execution of practical jokers.

Meantime, we are near primrose with the old type Dora Breadmore and James Grieve, and with the new type Clara Curtis, Primrose Spencer and Paradise Ivory.

Glorious are our blues. Who does not know and love the beautiful old hooded lavender, Lady Grizel Hamilton? That, with Countess of Radnor, Mrs. Higginson, Junior, Captain of the Blues and Navy Blue, held sway once upon a time. They lost their supremacy to Frank Dolby, Lord Nelson and A. J. Cook—beautiful Sweet Peas all, yet destined, perhaps, to wane before the rising stars of Masterpiece, Asta Ohn, Zephyr, and Lord Nelson Spencer. The veined blue Helen Pierce combines the attractions of beautiful colour, distinctiveness, and free blooming. We salute the Stars and Stripes with heartfelt gratitude for this lovely variety.

From veining to flaking is not a far stride, and it takes us into an even more spacious field of beauty. The old pink and rose flakes, Aurora, America, and Jessie Cuthbertson, retire to make way for waved forms, and dull must they be to the sense of beauty who do not do homage to Aurora Spencer, Mrs. Wilcox and Mrs. W. J. Unwin. Prince Olaf and Marbled Blue still stand as representatives of the blue flakes—a class in comparatively small demand.

We did not part from our old mauve, Dorothy Tennant, without a sigh, but with the newer Mrs. Walter Wright beside it there was no room for doubt—its day was done. Time, however, brought a dramatic revenge for the humiliated Dorothy. Driven, *passée*, from the stage to make way for a larger, brighter rival, she returns triumphant in a waved form, and as Tennant Spencer bids fair to revive all the triumphs of her youth. Thus does the Sweet Pea enjoy a power which poor humanity can only win, like Faust, at the cost of its soul.

In the days of the old plain-standards there was much shifting of places among the purples, violets and maroons. Stanley, Shahzada and Othello had their little hour, only to give way finally to Black Knight, that maroon whose glossy sheen eventually gave it undisputed pride of place. Until the great Spencer break-up came, Black Knight seemed destined to enjoy a long career of supremacy, but with the advent of the giant waved standards it was seen that it was only a matter of time before a maroon Spencer should supersede it. The maroon Spencer is here. It came first as Silas Cole, but that was unfixed. It followed as E. C. Mathews and Douglas Unwin. Prince of Asturias came between, and it is a good variety, of majestic size and rich colour, but it is not quite a self. There is a suspicion of chocolate in the standard, of violet in the wings. Many like it, and I do not seek to disparage a fine variety but merely to make it clear that it is not a maroon self.

How far we are from having exhausted the list of beautiful Sweet Peas we realise when we reflect that we have given no consideration yet to the edged and "Fancy" varieties. In the old days these were the weakest section of all, but that is not the case now that the Sweet Pea is Spencerised, and comprises yellow as well as white grounds. Dainty was a charming Pea, and long held sway among the Picotee-edged varieties, but the glorious Elsie Herbert, with its superior size and exquisite waving, came only to conquer.

We had no old-type flower to anticipate in colour the bordered yellow ground, of which the first to be shown were Evelyn Hemus and Mrs. Rothera, afterwards called Sutton's Queen. The former had only a pencilling of pink round the edge, the latter had a broad but not defined border. Mrs. C. W. Breadmore came to vie with Evelyn Hemus; and Mrs. Henry Bell, Mrs. Routzahn (from America), Gladys Burt, Syeira Lee and Mrs. Hugh Dickson with Sutton's Queen. In the days of my first edition Mrs. Routzahn and Syeira Lee remain unfixed. Gladys Burt and Mrs. Hugh Dickson are true, and they display a richness of colour on the edge, combined with beauty of form and large size, that renders them amongst the most charming of all Sweet Peas. Too broad a belt of colour is not wanted in this class. If it extended nearly to the centre it would come close to Constance Oliver, which only falls short of selfdom in showing a primrose heart.

Among the old Bicolors were Apple Blossom, Beacon and Triumph. Many growers remember the pretty, free-blooming Apple Blossom, with its rosy standard and blush wings. It lives again in the American waved variety Apple Blossom Spencer, and in a richer coloured form in Mrs. Andrew Ireland —a Pea of noble proportions and weighty substance. Triumph also has its waved or Spencer form.

Few of the old-type flowers had a more distinct form than Coccinea, the colour of which is cerise. Its shape was repeated in the ivory-hued May Perrett, with its brown calyx, and in the pearly pink Queen of Spain. The Coccinea Spencer is coming to the market at the time of publication. Chrissie Unwin and Cherry Ripe are near it in colour.

An author who sees what is being done on the grounds of the principal raisers must needs write with reservations. In raising Sweet Peas, as in wireless telegraphy and aeroplanes, all is in a state of development. The leading variety of one year is all but forgotten the next. Thrills and sensations are provided at every show, just as they are at the end of each instalment of a serial story. The fact that people were talking of finality before the first waved flower appeared should warn us to avoid the most distant hint of it now. I hope that an ever-growing multitude of readers will make many editions of this book necessary, and that as many changes in the Appendix will tell of the development that is going on.

There is but one prophecy that it is safe to make, and it is that the changes will be restricted to the flower. The fate of the Cupid and Bush Sweet Peas affords no encouragement to expect changes in the habit of the plant.

COTTAGE GARDENS.

[See Chapter XIII.]

The roof with its weather-worn thatching,
   The chimney-pile, crumbled and rent,
The eaves where young swallows are hatching,
   The gutter all tangled and bent,
The porch with its smother of Woodbine,
   The wall with its time-mellowed stain,
The byre with its mantle of Jasmine
   All come with the summer again.

I see, in the dreams of the winter,
   When the biting wind howls through the street,
And the rage of the storm tears to splinter
   The moonlight that pierces the sleet—
I see by the path of the cottage
   The border aglow with its bloom,
And the elder who creeps in his dotage
   Into sunshine from shade of the tomb.

I see the wild tangle of Roses
   A-swing on the frame of the arch,
I see the soft green that discloses
   The tenderest tint of the Larch.
I see the red Pæonies blending
   Their ripeness with youth of the Phlox,
While the heads of the white Pinks are bending
   To meet the caress of the Box.

I see the tall Larkspur upflinging
   Its blue to the blue of the sky,
I see the white Lily upspringing,
   And the Poppies blown in from the rye.
I see the Sweet Pea tendrils twining,
   Like baby hands clutching at space,
I see gay Geraniums shining,
   And the smile of the Pansy's bright face.

Oh, cottage homes, humble and lowly,
   The heart in its weariness turns
From the world, unillumed and unholy,
   To the hearths where your modest fire burns.
The soul that the fierce city hardens,
   And binds with a steel-riven chain,
Grows soft in the scent of your gardens,
   And bursts into freedom again.

CHAPTER XIII.

OF THE SWEET PEA IN ENGLISH COTTAGE GARDENS.

SWEET PEAS never seem to look happier than in the cottage garden. One might fancy that they had an innate sympathy for Hodge, and loved the intimate association of his Cabbages, his Onions, and his children.

Hodge himself has a way with them which they cannot resist. Not for him are the new-fangled ideas of sowing the seeds in frames, and cultivating the plants in pots before planting them in the garden. "Peas is Peas," and the place for them from the outset is the open garden. He does not prepare composts, drain pots, nurse and coddle. He would just as soon think of wrapping Mary Ann, aged seven, up in a blanket, and carrying her to school on a wet day. Mary Ann has got to trudge it, and sit the morning through with her little fat toes damp, while she acquires valuable practical information to help her through life, such as the date of the Norman Conquest, and the whereabouts of the watershed of the Euphrates. And Mary Ann, who ought to fall an early victim to rheumatic fever, grows up healthy and rosy, while the Sweet Peas flourish.

The fact is, Hodge is a gardener by instinct. Nearly everything that he handles grows, although it only gets the plainest of fare, because he has the knack of managing his soil properly. He knows when to work it, and when to keep away from it. He knows when it is right for sowing, and when it is not. He could not point out to you all the signs and tokens which guide him in his decisions, but he knows the right thing to do at the right time, and that goes a long way in gardening.

One of the great charms of the cottage flower garden is its irresponsibility. When the cottager arranges his vegetable crops he works on some sort of plan. There is a place for every crop, and the rows are as straight as gun barrels. But he has rarely any order with his flowers. Somehow, they never look as if they had been put in, but only as if they had grown. Note the patch of ground between the gate and the parlour window. It contains Asters, Stocks, Pansies, Pinks, Canterbury Bells and a standard Rose. The flowers chum together without a bit of formality. There has never been an exchange of cards. Every day is an At Home day with all of them. It would be thought hardly possible to get Sweet Peas in without smothering the other things, unless they were put in a straight row at the back, but Hodge manages it with a few clumps of sticks. The Peas drop in casually, are told to make themselves at home without any fuss, and straightway do so.

Sometimes one sees a row of Sweet Peas in a cottage garden sown in mixture. Is it not always a healthy row, a gay row? Do not the colours seem to blend naturally? Whoever saw a more pleasing row of Sweet Peas than Hodge's own? Taller plants, if you like, thicker stems, longer stalks, bigger flowers, but never a more delightful picture.

The cottager is more at home with mixed than with named Sweet Peas. It is true that the names are not quite so formidable as those of many Roses, particularly Roses of continental origin. Hodge is not staggered with "Souvenir de Maria Zozayas" or "Kaiserin Augusta Victoria." Most Sweet Peas have originated in England. But even Mrs. Hardcastle Sykes takes a little handling for a man who was worried with a dozen useless subjects during his time at the village school, and thankfully escaped at thirteen with doubtful ability to write his own name.

The cottager need never grow Sweet Peas under names unless he is cultivating them for show. He is right to consider his pocket, and save himself perplexity, by buying cheap mixed seed. But if he is an advanced man who makes a point of competing at the exhibitions he ought to know something about named varieties, because the schedule is likely to stipulate that there shall be six, twelve or more separate sorts sown. It is rarely compulsory to put name cards to the vases, but it is understood that judges (who are supposed to be capable of recognising every variety in existence at a glance, but are rarely anything of the kind) like to see them, and are influenced in their decisions by seeing considerable diversity of colours.

The village schoolmaster is often a good friend to the cottager in this matter of names. He will help with the labels when the seeds are sown, and with the cards when show days arrives—unless he happens to be secretary, in which case he will be in a highly worried and peppery state, owing to competitors breaking every regulation in the schedule, tent-contractors being late, judges missing their trains and the band wiring that it cannot come, because the conductor has contracted measles. In such extremity let the cottager think of his own Freddy, recently passed into the fifth standard, who will seat himself firmly on his prominent breeches patch, and with copious inking of fingers write out the names in a bold round hand, with no worse average than two spelling mistakes per card.

When the cottager thus grows Sweet Peas under names for exhibition, it is perhaps best that he should put them in separate clumps beside the garden path. They will have plenty of room there, and be easy to get at from the time that they are sown until the great day comes. They will get many a bucket of water, many a pailful of liquid manure, which they might not receive if they were in a more distant part of the garden.

A Cornish cottager crony of mine grows his prize Sweet Peas in a semi-circle round the midden. He lives in the same cottage that his grandfather had. The reader may have heard of Kenaz Rosewarne. He was a terrible fellow for a "wrastle." I have heard that Kenaz (whose portrait now adorns the wall just above the chimneypiece of the cottage) weighed eighteen stone, although only five feet six and a quarter inches high, and was so far round that when rivals appeared they took one good look at him, and then retired in despair of ever being able to span him. Michael Rosewarne is proud of his famous grandsire, but prouder still of the Sweet Peas that grow so luxuriantly with their roots in the rich soil around the midden. As he put it :—

" 'Tis well to be able to throw a man a clean fall, but I be not gifted that way. Happen I tried it I'd get thrawed myself, an' I rackon that any game where you gets the warst of it be a fule's game. When I was a young feller I went into no wrastling rings. I took one day off a year, and that was Helston Flora Day, when I danced the Furry dance with the young gells in and out o' the houses in Coinagehall Street and Meneage Street, and down by the Bowling Green in Helston town in May month."

Michael, we see, was for Flora from his youth up. His Sweet Peas make a screen for the midden, and win him prizes at summer shows.

If the average cottager has one failing with Sweet Peas it is to sow the seed too thickly. Michael Rosewarne is not guilty of that error. He puts his seeds just six inches apart, neither more nor less, and he sprinkles Hayle sand around them, because the gentleman who first encouraged him to grow Sweet Peas told him that Hayle sand was a sure preventive of the attacks of mice and birds, and so he had proved it.

Myself.—" Why not any other sand, Michael ? "

Michael.—" Because Hayle sand's say-sand to start with, and full o' small shell besides. No mice will come nigh it, nor birds, no, nor yet slugs when the plants are through the ground if only you sprinkle a bit o' Hayle sand round them."

Michael did not positively assert that other sea-sand would not serve the purpose equally as well as Hayle sand, provided it contained a good deal of fine shell; but he had grave doubts about it. He collected a supply of Hayle sand once a year, when he paid a visit to a brother in the fishery at St. Ives; and he told me how the fishermen made tea, which was to keep on adding fresh lots of tea leaves to the contents of the kettle (a teapot being regarded as a useless complication) without shaking the old ones out until the kettle got so full that a fresh start was absolutely necessary. A charged kettle had once been left unemptied when a mackerel boat was laid up for the season in Hayle river, and by great good fortune Michael was present when the boat was fetched out again, some months afterwards. Water was put on to the old leaves, the kettle was boiled, and a brew of " tay " was yielded the like of which Michael had never tasted before. The very thought of it, years afterwards, filled him with ecstacy.

Michael Rosewarne had a recipe for trapping slugs which was far remote from tea. If he found traces of slugs about his garden he placed small heaps of brewers' grains here and there, because he had found that they presented an irresistible attraction for slugs, which trooped as eagerly to the spoil as the continental fleas, of which Thackeray wrote, to the succulent Briton.

CHAPTER XIV.

OF THE SWEET PEA IN SCOTTISH GARDENS.

> Ower the border, ower and away,
> Eager and hot for the merry foray.
> No cattle to steal, no foemen to smite
> Mid clatter and yell in the dead of the night.
> But a boxful o' flowers in the shade of a tent,
> And a wee drap together when show day is spent,
> Scotsman or Southron, whichever may fa',
> Crying: Hey for the Thistle, Rose, Shamrock and a'.

THE reader is making, perhaps, for Abbotsford. He is fresh from the enchanting pages of Lockhart, and he wants to see the room where the Master, lighting his own fire and lamp early on winter mornings when all the household still slept, wrote his matchless romances and stirring verse. Shall I try to draw the reader away from such a pilgrimage? No, no, for thither I too have gone with reverential steps. But afterwards? If the objective is Edinburgh, why go through Galashiels, with its bare factories? Why not follow the Tweed eastward, even at the cost of some extra miles. Here come Melrose, and St. Boswells and Dryburgh, with their hallowed stones. The charm of the Tweed grows with every seaward mile. Awheel with valise, or afoot with knapsack, we ramble towards Berwick. Often the imperious road takes us high above the stream, and we see the water in flashes among green foliage and brown tree trunks. But in places it carries us down to narrow, grey, shambling bridges, over whose stained stones we lean and dream.

Anon we come to Kelso, where Tweed and Teviot meet, and smile up with foamy expansiveness at a clean white town that once knew all the stormy riot of border war, but now pursues a peaceful career of Turnip-growing. Still the cunning river lures us on, losing little of its influence until we reach Coldstream. Now we turn northward, though Flodden Field lies a few miles to the south. We have allowed ourselves to linger for a few hours under the spell of the past, in spite of its atmosphere of intrigue, violence and bloodshed, because of the overpowering personality of Scott. But Flodden has no charm with which to beguile us. We come back to the present. We draw in the fragrant breath of a peaceful countryside, we see the blossoms in the cottage gardens; and we realise that within a few miles of us lies that fertile valley under the shadow of the Lammermuir Hills wherein Sweet Peas grow with a luxuriance and a beauty of blossom that no other part of Scotland and few parts of England can equal.

The old town of Duns, once the county town of Berwickshire, is the centre of Scotland's Sweet Pea garden. The little villages of Fogo to the South, and Edrom to the North, vie with the gardens of Duns itself in producing gigantic and richly coloured Sweet Peas, as fresh, as healthy, as winsome, as the border maids. Visitors from the dry and burning south gaze in wonder at the marvellous Sweet Peas of Duns. The dull old town has grown bright and youthful again with the glory of its blossoms. Drowsing after its turbulent past, when the Armstrongs came from beyond the Cheviots with strong arms, sharp blades and no consciences worth mentioning, sometimes to drub the men of Duns and sometimes to be drubbed by them—drowsing on the memory of old-time melées, it suddenly awakened to the discovery that it possessed a soil and climate in which Sweet Peas luxuriated, and to find that its florists could give the Sassenach as shrewd a thrashing with flowers as ever their ancestors had done with pikes.

A few miles north-west from Coldstream brings us to Fogo. We make for the school, and in the Dominie's garden we find Sweet Peas of most amazing vigour—plants twelve feet high —plants with flower stems two feet long—plants covered with great flowers that have all the glowing freshness of a highland morning. We ejaculate another famous Dominie's favourite exclamation as we gaze. What size! What colour! Pro-dee-gi-ous!

We pass on to Nisbet, to Duns, to Edrom—still the same lofty stature, gigantic stems and gorgeous colouring. We ask ourselves if we ever saw Sweet Peas before. We revise our ideals, raise our standards. We draw forth our watch and lay the face upon one of the flowers, only to find that the flattened petals overlap its edges.

Of course, we lead the happy growers into selected corners, and extract the secrets of their culture. We find that they sow their seeds in autumn, winter the young plants in cool houses (keeping them dry) and put them out in spring in soil that has been dug three feet deep and interlarded with rich manure. All this and much more we learn, but it is not always that we find, after we have sown, wintered, and planted in deepened, highly manured land in our own garden, that our plants are as the plants of Duns, and our flowers as the flowers on which we gaze with such astonishment and delight when we come up out of the South into bonnie Scotland.

CHAPTER XV.

OF THE SWEET PEA IN WALES AND THE WEST COUNTRY.

In the broad moist western marches, where the ocean winds blow sweet,
And the dead years echo faintly to the tramp of Cymric feet,
Where the swift Atlantic surges send their salt-tinged breath to land,
And the shadowy mists drip goodness with a large and far spread hand,
There are gardens rich and fertile—gardens mellow with the scent
Of the Sweetbrier and the Hawthorn, and the Violets born in Lent,
Gardens golden, gay and gleaming when the Daffodils unclose,
Gardens radiant, ripe and ruddy with the Pæony and Rose.

There's the garden of the cottage, there's the garden of the mill,
There's the garden of the coastguard, shining white upon the hill,
There's the garden by the churchyard where the sombre Yew trees sleep,
And the garden of the herdsman on the down among the sheep.
There's the garden of the Welshman, there's the glebe of Somerset,
There's the fair Devonian homestead, where the winsome maids are met—
One and all of these bright gardens, by the heaving western seas,
Get their crowning charm and perfume from the dancing, glad Sweet Peas.

WOULD the Sweet Pea pilgrim see Sweet Peas in all the stature and majesty of their kinghood, let him go West.

In those gardens that are watered by a rainfall which ranges from forty to a hundred inches per annum, and where the generous loam lies deep, the plants grow with a lustihood of vigour that rejoices the grower's heart.

Every kind of plant is favoured by certain natural conditions. Where they exist the grower is like the happy cyclist who reels off the miles before a following wind and on a downward road; when they are absent he is like the yachtsman who has to "ratch and ratch" in the face of an adverse breeze.

Consider the tall growth, the long stems, the ramifying shoots, the many leaves, of the Sweet Pea. Does it not possess a very considerable evaporating surface? Must not its demands for moisture vastly exceed those of a small, fine-foliaged plant like a Carnation? We note these things and we acknowledge their force. We find ourselves face to face with plain physiological facts, and, accepting them frankly, we make certain deductions. We say that a plant which so plainly calls for so much moisture may be suited by districts where there is a heavy rainfall.

I have spent long, happy hours among the Sweet Peas of the Western gardens. It is good to see beautiful Sweet Peas anywhere, but it is best to see them at home, with the strong stems beneath them, and the green leaves as their setting. Beauty at the opera, with her snowy neck, her jewel-crowned hair, has something that suggests the distant, even the unapproachable. We admire from afar. We can see the laughing eyes, but not the love which lurks within their depths. Perhaps we feel a twinge of scepticism as to the reality of it all. We have heard of the secrets of the dressing room, and we fear that there may be something artificial at work. Beauty at home is real, and within our reach. It is companionable.

When one sees Sweet Peas at home in the West Country one see them at their best. In a Cornish garden ("Trevarrick") that I know there is a glory of Rhododendrons and Camellias in spring, and of Sweet Peas in the summer. The Rhododendrons are great trees, laden with huge trusses of crimson, rose, pink or white flowers. The Camellias spread into magnificent bushes, and are a mass of bloom in March and April. Seen in the soft light of a spring morning these glorious shrubs form a picture the recollection of which can never be effaced. But the Sweet Peas are as beautiful in their season. In the rich loamy soil and moist climate they grow eight to ten feet high, branch from the very base, flower early and low, and for many weeks bloom unweariedly.

And there is a Devonian garden, a few miles south of Exeter, the memory of which comes to me. With her rich red soils, almost as bright as the famous Potato lands of Dunbar and North Lincolnshire, and her heavy rainfall, the fair county of Devon can grow Sweet Peas with the best when she makes the attempt. There should be wholesome rivalry between her and her neighbours Dorset and Somerset. With such rich pastures as these two counties possess there must be favourable conditions for Sweet Peas. The pleasant little Dorsetshire town of Blandford produces Sweet Peas of the finest exhibition quality. Mr. Thomas Hardy's Wessex rustics will add new charms to their pretty thatched homesteads when they have learned how suitable Sweet Peas are for cottage gardens.

Wales has mighty growers of Sweet Peas. Let the reader who loves this beautiful flower, and at the same time admires magnificent scenery, make for the north-western marches. He is at Shrewsbury, perhaps? Then let him make a circuit north and west. Some ten miles due north of Shrewsbury will bring him to Wem, a little whity-brown stone town which is a very Mecca for Sweet Pea pilgrims. Here are the gardens of that great flower wizard, Henry Eckford, under whose patient hands the flower first learned to spread its wings. Who that knew him can ever forget Eckford? The stalwart figure, the noble, white-bearded face, the gentle voice, the tender hands, caressing alternately the lovely flowers which his genius had called into being and the grandchildren toddling at his knee—remain a green memory.

When this poor Scottish lad came south he had but one asset in the world—a deep interest in the improvement of flowers. He did not know what he was going to make experiments upon, for he loved them all. While pursuing his daily work as a professional gardener he began cross-fertilising Verbenas, and quickly added many beautiful new varieties to those which existed already. But the Verbena had begun to decline in public favour, and the time came when there was no longer a demand for novelties. Reluctantly he had to give up work on his old favourite. He was crossing other flowers, but it was only under strong pressure from circumstances that he abandoned the Verbena.

It was not long, however, before the Sweet Pea more than filled the vacant place. The early crosses yielded some charming new varieties, and the public speedily grew interested in them. Here there was double encouragement for the raiser. Henry Eckford pursued his labours with renewed ardour. He opened a new mine, and struck a lode of pure metal. Thenceforward to the end of his long life he produced an unceasing stream of exquisite new Sweet Peas. The appetite of the public grew on its dainty food. The Sweet Pea became a universal favourite. It found its way into every garden.

From Wem the pilgrim will bear westward, although still moving to the north. He will pass through pretty Ellesmere, with its spacious lake, and enter Wales near Overton, where the winding Dee flows at the foot of lofty banks and murmurs placidly over a rocky bed. In nearly every village between here and Wrexham he will find Sweet Peas during the summer—Sweet Peas eight feet high and more, with long stems, with huge flowers, with colours so fresh and lustrous that one might almost suppose that a new race had come into being in this favoured climate.

Why not such delightful flower pilgrimages as these? Tourists rush heatedly from place to place, choking in trains, suffocating in towns, gazing with ill-concealed weariness at pictures, statues and brasses, fondly imagining that they are acquiring "culture" and "a wider knowledge of art," when they are only learning how to become insufferable bores and pedants. The flower-lover has the countryside, the gardens, the cottages, the old country inns, the woods, the meadows, the streams for his entertainment.

From Wrexham he moves into Cheshire. My thoughts linger on a lovely garden a few miles from Chester (not far from the Shropshire border), where an amateur of means, taste and enthusiasm raises new Sweet Peas, and grows them magnificently. They fill beds, they fringe walks, best of all they cover old walls, to which they are trained on sticks. Sweet Peas are not generally looked upon as wall plants, nor, indeed, are they climbers, although they throw out tendrils with which to support themselves; but in this case they form a beautiful mantle for a lofty garden wall, reaching to a height of quite ten feet, and bearing splendid flowers on long stems.

This system of culture reminds me to raise a protest against the accepted idea that Sweet Peas are only suitable for the open. I have myself grown them successfully on wooden trellis-work, and a Hertfordshire gardener grew a beautiful lot on the netting enclosing a fruit plantation.

Sweet Peas thrive in the Lake Country, of course. In that humid climate they are favoured by one of the most important factors in success—atmospheric moisture. Carnforth, which is on the threshold of the lake country, enjoys a reputation for its Sweet Peas as great as Banbury for its cakes. And Ulverston is a famous centre for our beautiful flower.

CHAPTER XVI.

OF THE SWEET PEAS IN IRISH GARDENS.

Fair Sovereign who robs of stern nature her frown !
Green fields are your throne and gay flowers are your crown,
Your pastures are matchless, your gardens are famed
For a richness that leaves other gardens ashamed.
Seek wealth in the Tulip, Narcissus, Sweet Pea
And no longer unfruitful your labours can be.
When England is bare' mid the smoke of her mills,
You will send her the flowers from your valleys and hills.

Sweet island of flowers, once a land of unrest,
No longer your peasants shall fly to the West.
No longer in squalor your children shall lie,
No longer in hovels your elders shall die.
Fertility's hand shall be laid on your soil,
Prosperity's blessing shall guerdon your toil ;
For the land is your people's, and Nature has given
To freshen your crops the moist largesse of heaven.

IN a mid-September day I enter a hall in the heart of London to see a show of Roses. Where do the principal prizes go ? To Ireland ! Those magnificent stands, full of flowers of huge size, splendid substance and rich colour, have come from the Green Isle. The flowers of the English growers who fight out the principal competitions in July are as the products of suburban amateurs by comparison with the wonderful Irish blooms two months later.

We do not have great Sweet Pea shows in September, not because it is impossible to get good flowers then, but because the trade growers have allowed their plants to ripen in order to be able to supply amateurs with seed for the following year. If we did have late Sweet Pea exhibitions—if this problem of seed (which does not affect Rose growers) were non-existent—who can doubt that Ireland would distinguish herself as greatly with Sweet Peas as she does with Roses ? Not, assuredly, he who has seen the Irish flower gardens in the full richness of their September splendour. The mild climate, the abundant rainfall, give the gardens a wonderful glow and freshness. Under a kindly September sun they burst into a great crash of beauty.

Sweet Pea culture is spreading in Ireland. We must not expect to find so many amateurs there as in England—remember that the population of Ireland is only about one-tenth that of the " predominant partner "—and when we glance through the A's in the members' list of the National Sweet Pea Society, we are not surprised to find that there are fewer members in all Ireland than there are in Surrey alone. But if the increase is not rapid it exists, especially near the principal towns. Sweet Pea growers multiply apace around Dublin, around Belfast, around Cork. These great cities are famous for the beauty of their gardens, and the Sweet Pea helps to give them that beauty.

It will spread faster still when the work of the Department of Agriculture and Technical Instruction, has developed. When Pat has a decent cottage and a bit of ground, and has listened to illustrated lectures on gardening, he will want to have flowers around him; he will no longer be satisfied with a bare and filthy yard. In the years to be he will be England's market gardener. He will send her fruit, vegetables and flowers. He will add to her food supply over narrow seas that an enemy's cruisers cannot menace. He has a huge market at his gates. With his fertile soil and favourable climate he can extend the area of his nurseries and seed grounds with the confidence that there is a profitable trade awaiting him.

Meanwhile, there is a band of Sweet Pea amateurs spread over Ireland. We find them in County Kildare (particularly at Naas), in County Meath, in Queen's County, in County Armagh, in County Louth, in County Carlow, in Limerick, in County Westmeath, in County Wexford, in County Antrim, in County Down, in Kilkenny, in County Dublin, in County Wicklow, and in County Tyrone. It is not a large band, but it is a keen one, and its influence will spread rapidly as the years pass on.

CHAPTER XVII.
OF THE SWEET PEA IN THE BRITISH COLONIES.

Here's a cheer for the flower, and a cheer for the flag
(There are red, white and blue in the seedsman's dull bag).
Where the Peas climb the sticks and the Jack mounts the pole
It's England and home—we are one heart and soul.
Beyond the snows of the north and the warm southern seas
The folds of our ensign flow out on the breeze;
And the scent of our flowers in the wilds of the earth
Brings back to the exile the sweet land of his birth.

MEMORY plays us strange tricks at times. We have got to the halfway stage of life, perhaps, and we see things through a haze. There is a certain old village in faraway England—a village that once we knew. We like to think of it now and then, and to wonder if it is still the same, while we grow our tea in Ceylon, shear our sheep in New Zealand, prune our Apple trees in Columbia, sow our wheat in Canada, cord our wool in Australia, or mine our gold in South Africa.

In the early years of our Colonial life that village in the old country stood out sharp and clear, as St. Ives stands out from its Cornish seas at dead of winter, every detail distinguishable. There was the square tower of the church, looming in grey solidity among the beeches; the brown roof of the Rectory, with its ivy-clad gables; the great tithe barn, with its lichen-stained walls; the forge with its tumbled roof; the school that emitted a dull droning, as of some monstrous hive, in the morning hours, and at noon suddenly emitted a whooping horde of children; the house near the pond, with the Cedars beside it, where she who caused such turmoil in our youthful breast lived with a gang of awkward, lumbering brothers. A year or two ago we remembered it all. But time has passed, and the haze has grown up. We remember that something was cleared away near the village green, and we are not quite sure whether it was the tithe barn or the stocks. Were the Cedars really Cedars, or were they Wellingtonias? She married, we have heard, or was it her sister—the sister with whom we squabbled perpetually?

We are loth to let the old village go, but bit by bit it is slipping away. We cling to it, but unavailingly. There are moments when we look back to it with a sudden, unexplainable yearning; can it really be that once when we looked into the millstream there we saw a fresh young face with a tangle of brown hair?

The haze grew thicker year by year, as our hair grew greyer and thinner, but one day it disappeared, and we saw the village again just as it was on the day that we left it. The mist of the years went out, as the mist sometimes goes off the sea, quite suddenly. A new chum had sent us a bunch of Sweet Peas, and the scent of them—the same scent as that which always hung around the garden of the Cedars (we remember quite well that they were cedars now) during summer—had achieved this miracle. Old village! old flowers! If a lump tries to grow up in our throats that we insistently choke down it only means that we still love you.

We love you, and we will not let the memory of you pass away. We will keep it green with some of the old flowers from England, the fragrance of which shall bring back the happy days of youth, and keep our outlook on life fresh, cheerful and hopeful. We had not realised how arid our hearts were growing amid the unwholesome dust-shower of our rush for wealth until those Sweet Peas came.

We had not noticed how often pessimistic reflections and cynical criticisms escaped our lips. We had not remarked how rapidly the pile was wearing off the world's carpet, and how threadbare the latter was becoming. But we had noticed that the years were passing, and that as each slipped away our interest in life lessened.

To the writer in England there come many letters from overseas which tell of the craving of Colonials for sweet English flowers. And not a few of the correspondents—dear, trustful souls—send sums of money to a person of whom they know nothing except through his books, to be transmitted to some approved florist or seedsman for the purchase of flowers. They make anxious inquiries about transit, fearing injury to the seeds from bilge-water and change of climate. There is no need for apprehension. Every seedsman of standing knows how to pack seed for export. He has his damp-proof paper and his air-tight boxes. Even if the wicked stevedore were to throw every box of seeds into the deepest depths of the hold (which he does not do, of course) the seeds would be safe. The stowaway could sit upon the box in tender melancholy, while he chewed his lump of hemp and, drawing a narrow subsistence from this unappetising fare, weep for his mother.

Many Colonials send letters about Sweet Peas, and some send unmounted photographic prints of their flowers. Here is a budget from New Zealand, which contains a garden scene. How mindful of home! There are tall columns of bloom, towering over stalwart figures, and there are smiling British faces, from which beams a wholly pardonable pride in the flowers beside them. The scene might almost as well be Addlestone as Taranaki.

The New Zealander who comes home tells us that the Islands will grow everything, and so, of course, they will grow Sweet Peas. The soil is fertile, the climate is equable, and there is adequate but not excessive moisture. In so favoured a climate it would be strange indeed if so free-growing and adaptable a plant as the Sweet Pea did not thrive. Macaulay himself did not know it, but the principal question in the mind of the New Zealander standing amid the ruins of London will be whether the aeroplane service to the Essex flower seed grounds is suspended or not. He has come over for the latest Sweet Pea novelties, and—for your New Zealander is nothing if not pertinacious—he means to get them.

Australia is taking to Sweet Peas. While her statesmen build up navies for the defence of the Commonwealth in the stormy years that are supposed to be ahead (but which will be years of peace instead when the nations have become civilised by the love of flowers), while her great towns breed cricketers capable of whipping the Old Country, her rural folk cultivate the all-popular flower. Perhaps her climate, so favourable to good wickets and fast scoring, is a little too dry in the main to suit Sweet Peas perfectly; but amateurs are not to be baffled altogether, even by so potent a factor as climate.

This morning's post brings a letter from Camperdown, Victoria, which tells me of spreading interest there. In England it is odd to read a paragraph like this: "The seeds were sown in pots in March and the seedlings transplanted at the end of May. They do not make much growth *through the winter*, but they flower in November. We have about eight weeks of bloom provided that the sun does not get too fierce, and they seed very freely." Of course, our summer is the Australian winter.

South Africa has sent us many beautiful bulbs, and we have sent her the Sweet Pea in exchange. In her fertile soils, and under her sunny skies, it flourishes amazingly. It is spreading fast into the most distant corners of the united colonies, and the future fights of Briton and Boer will be in the show tent.

"East is East and West is West," but the twain have one common interest, and that is in their love for Sweet Peas. There, if there only, they can meet. India loves the flower, and is eager to get all the best varieties from the seedsman. Canada wonders if she has time, amid the rush of her development, to grow Sweet Peas, and, wondering, succumbs to its charms.

Sweet Peas are grown in all parts of Nova Scotia. The climate is suitable, as there is abundance of sunshine, yet it is never excessively hot in the daytime and the nights are cool. Halifax is the principal centre of culture, as there is a magnificent public garden in that favoured town. Almost everybody who has a garden in Nova Scotia grows Sweet Peas.

Letters about Sweet Peas come from British Columbia, from Newfoundland, from Jamaica, from the Bermudas, from Burmah, from the Gold Coast, from New Guinea, from St. Helena—wherever British people settle gardens come into being, and wherever gardens rise Sweet Peas grow.

CHAPTER XVIII.

OF THE SWEET PEA IN THE UNITED STATES OF AMERICA.

> It's a far, far cry to San Francisco
> From London town where the Plane trees grow;
> And if you go by Magellan's Strait
> It's a weary steam to the Golden Gate.
> But the land that once flung gold in showers
> To-day is a glorious land of flowers,
> And no thought lives of the angry seas
> 'Mid the league-long lines of the gay Sweet Peas.

THE British globe trotter who has visited Japan and Australia will often make his way homeward by California. From the land of the Golden Fleece to the Golden Gate! That town of glamour, San Francisco, attracts him irresistibly. Tales of the old gold-digging days haunt him. There is the fascination of the gigantic, the bizarre, the cosmopolitan, about 'Frisco. It is a town of stupendous things. Destroyed one year, it is rebuilt the next at a cost of £40,000,000. Of course he visits it. And then, perhaps, he hears about the flower farms, goes to see them, and makes a discovery. The California of the gold-digger he knew of, the California of the fruit-grower he knew of, but these vast spaces of Sweet Peas—miles upon miles of vivid colour, endless acres of brilliant bloom, filling the air with fragrance—these he had not known of.

California is becoming the world's great Sweet Pea garden. England, as well as America, draws from her. When the Sweet Pea lover goes into Essex, Cambridgeshire and Norfolk, and sees the large Sweet Pea farms, he will tell himself that here, surely, are being grown seeds enough to supply the whole country. Of a limited number of special varieties—perhaps novelties, perhaps sorts which loom largely on the show boards—yes; of the rank and file of sorts which are grown in every garden up and down the countryside—no. These cheap, popular things, often sold in fifty-seed packets for a penny or two, have to be grown by the ton in a climate where free-seeding can be relied upon, and in places where cheap labour is available. California has these conditions, England has not. These great, plump seeds of Sadie Burpee, of Navy Blue, of Miss Willmott, of Phenomenal, which gratify you so much, my amateur friend, by their size and freshness (you can actually see the huge, rollicking plants and bushels of flowers which they will produce in your mind's eye)—those seeds were not grown in Essex, Cambridgeshire, or Norfolk: they were grown in California.

It would not pay a British trader to grow these popular "lines" himself, even if he could rely upon a hot, dry summer for his harvest; which he cannot do, by any means. Taking bad seasons with good into consideration, he can buy them cheaper than he can grow them; and so, like the practical, hard-headed man that he is, he turns his attention to special sorts, of which less seed is wanted, and of which the price is higher.

The Californian seed grower has had two blessings bestowed upon him by a beneficent Providence: the first a summer that is always hot and dry; the second—John Chinaman. The sun ripens the seed, and John gathers it. He places no exorbitant value upon himself. He works hard and long for a low wage. The two assets put the English seed grower at a disadvantage. Even if he tried to get on level terms by importing John he could not import the sun with him.

Californian seed is nearly always good for the variety. It is as large as seed of the particular sort can be expected to be. It is thoroughly ripe. It germinates well. You may take six seeds out of a packet and find that they fall almost to powder under a sharp hammer stroke, but the remaining seeds speedily prove their vitality when sown.

British growers do not complain of the quality of Californian seed, but they do sometimes grumble at the want of truth of Californian stocks. There is no trouble with the old varieties which are quite fixed, but with the newer sorts that ought to be fixed there is often cause for lamentation. The Californian seed grower tells you that he has pulled out all the rogues which appeared in them. What has happened is that he has told John Chinaman to pull them out, and John has not done it. He has perhaps pulled off a part of the rogue, with the first flowers, and left the remainder. As the plants are mostly grown unsupported, it is easier to leave a portion of the plant than when the crop is on sticks or wire. Sometimes it is not the rogue which is pulled out, but an entirely inoffensive plant next to it. The rogue then goes

IN THE UNITED STATES OF AMERICA.

to seed and befouls the stock. We applaud John for the splendid seed he sends us, but we shake a warning finger at him for this careless rogueing. Let him look to it. Let him mend his ways. If it costs a little more to produce seed when the plants are supported we will pay it cheerfully, so long as we can be sure of getting true stocks.

California grows nearly 1,000 acres of Sweet Peas for seed. Think of it, 1,000 acres of Sweet Peas! What a wonderful colour effect must be produced! What vivid armies of scarlet, what tender breadths of cream and rose, what brilliant clouds of blue, what snowdrifts of white! Fields of Sweet Peas stretching away to the horizon, with the orange and salmon and apricot of Helen Lewis, Henry Eckford and Mrs. Henry Bell blending with the beautiful shades of sunset! As the sea takes its tint from the clouds above, so we might fancy the waves of Lady Grizel Hamilton, Lord Nelson and Flora Norton glistening with a new brilliance under the rich colour of the Western skies.

America has taken many beautiful Sweet Peas from England but she has given some splendid varieties in return. Let us tabulate a few of her gifts to us:—

Admiration.	Janet Scott.
America.	King Edward Spencer.
Apple Blossom Spencer.	Lottie Hutchins.
Asta Ohn.	Modesty.
Aurora Spencer.	Mrs. G. Higginson, Junior.
Blanche Ferry.	Mrs. Routzahn.
Cupid.	Navy Blue.
Dainty	Othello Spencer.
Earliest Sunbeams.	Phenomenal.
Flora Norton Spencer.	Senator Spencer.
Gorgeous.	Stella Morse.
Helen Pierce.	Tennant Spencer.

These two dozen new and old Sweet Peas comprise some magnificent sorts. America, Apple Blossom Spencer, Asta Ohn, Aurora Spencer, Dainty, Gorgeous, Helen Pierce, King Edward Spencer, Navy Blue and Tennant Spencer all made a most favourable impression on British growers when they first came over. Note among the twenty-four, too, the little Cupid, the old early Blanche Ferry, and the once popular pink Janet Scott.

American and British raisers have more than once produced the same variety at almost the same time. Thus, Burpee of Philadelphia, and House of Westbury-on-Trym, near Bristol, got a rich, bright, deep blue out of Navy Blue at practically the same time. The American raiser called his Brilliant Blue, the English specialist gave his the mighty name of Lord Nelson; the two proved to be identical. Then followed one of the most magnanimous acts ever performed in connection with a popular flower. Although Burpee had introduced the parent, Navy Blue, and might be said to have an inherited right in its offspring, he readily conceded to the English raiser the priority. But indeed, the American raisers have ever shown a generous spirit with regard to the question of priority in names, readily bowing to the decisions of the British National Sweet Pea Society. This has prevented what must otherwise have become a most troublesome state of confusion.

Although Sweet Pea improvement on a systematic scale began in England before it commenced in America, the first wave of popular enthusiasm for the flower started in the United States; and the early Eckford novelties sold much more largely in America than they did in the land of their birth. The American amateur enthusiast and writer, the Rev. W. T. Hutchins, the great seedsmen Burpee, Farquhar, Henderson, Morse, and Vaughan, have stamped their names indelibly on Sweet Pea history in America. All of these exercised influence on the progress of the Sweet Pea. The majority of the best novelties bear the familiar names of Burpee and Morse.

About the time of the British Bi-centenary celebration in 1900 American development sustained a setback, owing to trouble from a fungus, but the cloud passed, and progress was resumed.

America, led, too, with winter-blooming varieties. These are a very popular class with her, and a source of profit to her growers.

She sent us the Bush and Cupid sections, but British growers hardly find that they have a use for them. The Cupids are charming when full of bloom, but they are so prone to cast their buds that it is exceptional to see them well flowered in England. We do not always like the "tall" things of America best, but in the case of her Sweet Peas we do. Let her live up to her highest reputation for the gigantic in raising Sweet Peas. Expansive ideas will never prove too grandiose when they find expression in new and improved forms of this beautiful flower.

CHAPTER XIX.

OF WOMAN'S INFLUENCE ON THE SWEET PEA.

We need her for her patience, we need her for her taste,
    We need her for her hope when we are down,
We need her in the weary search for seeds that we've misplaced,
    And we need her at the show when judges frown.
We need her in the dairy, we need her in the ward,
    We need her at the play and at the ball,
We need her when a fretful babe has struck a midnight chord,
    But we need her in the garden most of all!

We need her for our Daffodils, because she always thinks
    Of planting ways that discord never mars.
We need her for our Roses, we need her for our Pinks,
    Because her colour-blending never jars.
We need her for Chrysanthemums, which, in the autumn hours,
    Revive our drooping spirits when they fall.
In fact we really need her for all our favourite flowers,
    And we need her for the Sweet Peas most of all!

WHEN a political question is being fought out those who read the arguments of the contending parties might readily believe, if they did not know better, that every member of the community is absorbed in that particular matter. The real truth generally is that the nation as a whole takes very little interest in it, and merely allows itself to be diverted by such humour as there may happen to be in the fray.

Shall I be accused of inaccuracy if I say that the majority of women are more interested in Sweet Peas than in the Suffrage? Pray, ladies of the Union, do not conclude from this that it is necessary to send a deputation to me to convince me of the justice of your cause. That would be entirely supererogatory. Besides, it would be bad for the deputation. Having speedily convinced it, by irrefragable evidence, that I was in no need of salvation, I should lead it into my Sweet Pea garden, and, politically speaking, its doom would be sealed. There would be a simultaneous outbreak of rapturous exclamations, an excited snatching forth of notebooks, and the deputation would be a deputation no more. It would have resolved into its components, each of whom would be scribbling down the names of the varieties and clamouring eagerly for hints on cultivation. And next morning, when the heads of the Union sat grimly awaiting its report, the deputation would be scattered all over the country at Sweet Pea shows.

Woman has already made her mark on Sweet Peas, just as she has on books. You, unhappy novelist, whose MS. has been returned by a dozen publishers in succession, may fume and fret, but why kick against the pricks? Are those publishers not advised by professional "readers?" And are not those professional "readers" aware that more than ninety per cent. of the people who read novels are women? Go to, my dear lad, you have not written what she wants; you have written what *you* want. Try again.

Raisers of Sweet Peas who want to make money are in somewhat the same position as novelists. They have to produce what the public wants, and the Sweet Pea public, like the novel-buying public, is largely composed of women. The father, the husband or the brother may actually write the cheque which accompanies the order, but the hand that guides the pen is that of the daughter, the wife, or the sister.

It is not the influence of the men who win the great prizes at exhibitions which dominates Sweet Peas, but the influence of quiet, unobtrusive women who never take a Sweet Pea farther away from their gardens than their drawing-rooms.

Ask a market grower what Sweet Peas are most in demand, and he will give you the names of a few sorts, the colours of which you will find to be pink, scarlet, or white.

Ask the seedsman what varieties he sells most of, and he will name varieties among which pink, scarlet, and white predominate.

Are prizes won through the marked effect of the pink, scarlet or white varieties in the stand? No! Judges make their awards on the size, substance and freshness of the flowers. It follows, therefore, that it is not the influence of the exhibitor which makes pink, scarlet, and white sell in such predominating quantities.

The reason why they are in such demand is that they show up well under artificial light, and are therefore particularly good for room decoration. Now, as it is woman who chooses the material for beautifying the home, the point is triumphantly established that the influence of woman dominates the Sweet Pea world. Nothing, indeed, could be more convincing. Exhibitors may protest, but they are overwhelmed by unalterable facts. The cold logic of the market garden and seed shop reduces them to a subordinate position, and exalts their daughters, wives and sisters.

When I dip back into the past I find no small amount of

evidence in favour of my next contention, which is that the Sweet Pea owes the extraordinary popularity which it enjoys now far more to woman's influence than to man's. When the late Henry Eckford began to produce his novelties, exhibitors took very little notice of them. Committees of horticultural societies looked at them, said "rather nice," and passed on to something else. Little enough of encouragement did the grand old florist receive from them. But wherever he showed his flowers there was a cluster of admiring women eager to scribble down names, and to prod their husbands and their gardeners into some show of interest in the new flower.

Have you ever noticed how feminine names, or names embodying feminine qualities, predominate among the older Sweet Peas? Recall Lady Grizel Hamilton, Countess of Radnor, Duchess of Sutherland, Princess Beatrice (long the most popular of all market varieties), Sadie Burpee, Blanche Burpee, Dorothy Eckford, Mrs. Walter Wright, Lovely, Modesty, Queen Victoria and Queen Alexandra. It was not alone the innate courtliness of his nature that made Eckford give his Sweet Peas feminine names, it was in part the encouragement that he received from women which influenced him. And the tendency continued when the waved type of flower came into existence: Countess Spencer, Gladys Unwin, Mrs. Hardcastle Sykes, Etta Dyke, Clara Curtis, Elsie Herbert, Evelyn Hemus, Audrey Crier, Nora Unwin and Nancy Perkin continued the tale of beautiful Sweet Peas with feminine names.

There is so much of arduous physical work connected with growing Sweet Peas for exhibition—so much trenching, wheeling of manure, staking and other laborious tasks—that we cannot look for woman to hold her own with men except in one department—that of decoration. Here it is taste that scores, not muscle, and here consequently, we find her supreme. The classes for decorated dinner tables and epergnes which form so charming a feature of Sweet Pea shows give woman her chance, and nobly she avails herself of it. (Let it be whispered that she also eagerly seizes on any chance of admonishing a judge who has only placed her second or third. But if it comes to that, is hers the only sex which considers the first prize a special prerogative?)

Sweet Peas are only grown to be gathered. Abstain from gathering them and the plants run to seed, and so lose their beauty. It sounds paradoxical, but it is only by taking the flowers off a Sweet Pea that we can make a good garden plant of it. By gathering Sweet Peas regularly woman showed that it could be made a good garden plant. Man did not make this discovery, he never would have done. Except when he was young and in love, and wanted a few flowers for his inamorata, he would never take the trouble to gather Sweet Peas—unless, indeed, he saw a way of making something out of them at a show, and in the early days of Sweet Pea development it was not a show flower. He would not spend an hour in gathering Sweet Peas, and another in arranging the flowers in his rooms. He would say that his time was too valuable for such trivialities. (Of course, he would spend any length of time in cutting up tobacco for rolling cigarettes.) Woman, therefore, at one and the same time proved the beauty of the Sweet Pea for room decoration, and its value as a garden plant. In a word, she made it. When she had done it man came along, formed a society, organised exhibitions, got his name inscribed on challenge trophies, and by these and other means usurped the leading position.

There is no flower so peculiarly a woman's as the Sweet Pea. Given a little help (such as any sturdy labourer will provide) in trenching and manuring the ground and in sharpening and forcing in the sticks, she can perform every cultural detail with ease. The sowing of the seed, whether in pots or in the open ground; the setting out of the plants if they have been raised under glass, the blending of colours, the tying, the stopping, the training—all these are light and agreeable tasks. The plant is not coarse, rough and spiny; it is soft, clinging, delicate and smooth. It is gentle, pure and sweet. In short, it possesses all the attributes that give woman herself her charm and influence.

We look to woman for many useful services with the Sweet Pea—for the suppression of monstrosities in shape and atrocities in colour, for lessons in the tasteful use of the flower, for persistent evidence of its value in the home. She has taught us already that it is the best of all garden flowers for filling vases, for decorating the dinner-table, and for imparting cheerfulness and grace to the drawing-room.

In some directions her influence is active, in others passive, but it is always an influence for good. We cannot do without it among Sweet Peas, and we are not going to try. We know that we can have it for the asking. Woman will no more be satisfied with a garden that contains no Sweet Peas than with a novel which lacks love. You see, she knows what really counts in this world.

CHAPTER XX.

THE SWEET PEA GROWER'S A.B.C.
A BIOGRAPHY, GUIDE AND SUMMARY.

> To the Artist his Art, to the workman his wages,
> To the gardener the flowers that are named in my pages.
> I tell you the tale of the flower and the man,
> Be blind to its faults as the chapters you scan.
> Just think of the blossoms—the old and the new—
> And think of the florist who carried them through ;
> The factors and facts, after all, make the story,
> Put writers aside, and give workers the glory.

IN a series of paragraphs, placed in alphabetical order, I give brief particulars of the men who have been mainly instrumental in developing the Sweet Pea, and a summary of the cultural and descriptive information which this work contains.

Aldersey, Hugh, of Aldersey Hall, Chester. Head of an old Cheshire county family. Having a great love of flowers he developed the garden at Aldersey Hall in a remarkable way, making it one of the most beautiful in the west of England. Giving special study to Sweet Peas he made many crosses, and raised the varieties Syeira Lee, Ruby, Scotch Pearl, Tortoiseshell, Topaz, Amethyst and Helen Grosvenor amongst others. All the varieties raised by him are distinguished by the breadth and substance of the standard.

America, United States of.—There is close communion between the United States and Great Britain in respect to Sweet Peas. Both of the great English-speaking nations are lovers of the flower. America has produced many beautiful varieties, notably Asta Ohn, True Lavender, America, Aurora, Helen Pierce, Dainty, Flora Norton Spencer, Tennant Spencer, King Edward Spencer and Aurora Spencer. She gave us the bush and Cupid sections. 'In the dry and sunny climate of California Sweet Peas are grown for seed on an immense scale. The seed produced there is of the finest quality, and well adapted for British gardens. Probably

California is destined to become the principal source of the world's supply of Sweet Pea seed, which must necessarily attain to gigantic proportions in the near future. See Chapter XVIII., also a paper on Sweet Pea growing in America by Mr. S. B. Dicks, in the National Sweet Pea Society's Annual for 1909.

Annual.—The National Sweet Pea Society's Annual is a publication of great interest and value to lovers of Sweet Peas, and, being published at a low price, comes within the means of every grower. Each issue contains articles by experts, the latest information as to novelties, a classification of the best varieties in their colours, and a list of Too-much-alike varieties.

Annuals.—The Sweet Pea (*Lathyrus odoratus*) is classed with the flowers known as hardy annuals, which grow from seed, flower and ripen their next crop of seed in the course of a year. No one will quarrel with the assertion that the Sweet Pea is the most beautiful, valuable and important of all the hardy annuals. As a class, the hardy annuals are particularly valuable to flower lovers of limited means, as the seed is cheap and the culture inexpensive.

Arkwright, Rev. Edwyn.—Of Télemly, Algiers, developed a class of winter flowering Sweet Peas, known as the Télemly strain. The flowers are small, and the range of colours is not great, but the plants are useful to those who want winter bloom. For further particulars see Chapter X.

Artificial Manures.—The chemical or artificial manures are capable of doing good service to the Sweet Pea grower. They may be used as supplementary to natural manure, or as a substitute for it. Probably the most vigorous growth is got from the use of yard manure, but artificials are particularly valuable for seed production. Basic slag (yielding phosphoric acid) and kainit (yielding potash) may be used in autumn at the rate of ten pounds and four pounds per rod respectively, where there has been trouble from eelworm, white-worm and root-rot. Superphosphate of lime (yielding phosphoric acid) and sulphate of potash (yielding potash) may be used at the rate of four and three pounds per rod respectively in early spring. If the plants are being grown for seed those fertilisers may be supplemented with half-a-pound of sulphate of iron. Nitrate of soda (yielding nitrogen) may be scratched lightly into the soil along the rows in May at the rate of an ounce per yard if the plants are not growing vigorously, but it must not be placed in contact with the plants. Superphosphate, phosphate of potash and nitrate of potash may all be used to form liquid manure. One ounce per gallon of water will be of sufficient strength. For fuller particulars of the use of artificial manures see Chapters V. and XI.

Audit.—An audit of the varieties of Sweet Peas exhibited at the principal show is generally one of the most interesting features of the National Sweet Pea Society's Annual. It shows the relative positions of the Varieties, and is therefore a useful guide to exhibitors.

Bakers.—A firm of florists and seedsmen at Wolverhampton, large growers of Sweet Peas, and introducers of the varieties Mrs. C. Mander, Mrs. Charles Foster, Bakers' Scarlet, Earl of Plymouth, Mrs. R. M. Shelton, Mrs. T. G. Baker and others.

Bath, R. H., Ltd.—Large florists and seedsmen at Wisbech, Cambridgeshire, who specialise Sweet Peas, and have been particularly identified with the introduction of many of the best American varieties. They have extensive trials of Sweet Peas every year. Raisers of Azure Fairy, Perdita, Distinction, and other varieties.

Bathurst, R.—Of Chudleigh, Devonshire. An amateur grower of Sweet Peas, who raised Devonshire Cream, Finetta Bathurst and other varieties.

Bell & Bieberstedt.—Seedsmen at Leith, Scotland. Introducers of Mrs. Bieberstedt.

Bicentenary.—The Bicentenary of the introduction of the Sweet Pea into Great Britain was celebrated by a great show at the Crystal Palace in 1900. Sweet Pea lovers attended from all parts of the world, and a magnificent display of flowers rewarded them. A report of the proceedings was published by the Committee of the Celebration, which subsequently developed into the National Sweet Pea Society.

Biffen, R. H.—Of Cambridge University. An amateur grower and raiser of Sweet Peas on Mendelian lines. Raised Zephyr, and other varieties.

Birds.—Often troublesome to Sweet Pea growers, either by eating the seed or pecking off the buds. For methods of prevention see Chapter XI.

Bolton, Robert.—A trade grower at Warton, Carnforth, and introducer of some of the most beautiful varieties, notably Mrs. Hardcastle Sykes, Mrs. Henry Bell, Kitty Clive, George

Baxter, Mrs. Watson, Triumph Spencer, Charles Foster and Clara Curtis.

Bowls.—See "Rooms."

Breadmore, C. W.—A trade grower at Winchester, Hampshire, who was one of the first to distinguish himself as an exhibitor. Introducer of many famous varieties, notably Prince of Asturias, Dazzler, Princess Juliana, Mrs. C. W. Breadmore, Elsie Herbert, Kathleen Macgowan, Snowflake, Audrey Crier, Marjory Linzee, King Alfonso, Helen Lewis, Countess of Northbrook, Etta Dyke and George Herbert.

Bridgeford, J. M.—Of Cricklewood, London. Served on the Floral Committee of the National Sweet Pea Society. An expert trade grower.

Buds.—The buds of Sweet Peas are an interesting study, particularly to the cross-fertiliser, because the sexual organs are mature in the bud. This being so it is important to make any crosses before the flower opens naturally. Bees sometimes pierce the flowers, and they have a way of depressing the keel and exposing the pollen, which they carry off, but in spite of this cross-fertilisation is rare, as the flowers are self-fertilised before outside agencies can come into play. The subject is discussed fully in Chapter III. Growers sometimes complain about the buds dropping off, but as a rule this trouble only occurs with the early buds. Extremes of drought and wet, or a dose of very strong liquid manure, may cause it. The Cupids are very prone to casting their buds under any conditions of culture, and this has had much to do with their fall into disfavour.

Bunting, G. A. & Co.—Seed growers and merchants at Bucknall Street, London, W.C. Introducers of Mrs. Walter Carter.

Burpee, W. Atlee, & Co.—Seedsmen in a very large way of business at Philadelphia, U.S.A., doing an enormous trade in Sweet Peas. They have been the chief means of many varieties being introduced to Great Britain; indeed, most of those named under "America" come through this great firm, also Primrose Spencer, White Spencer, Brilliant Blue (Lord Nelson), Mrs. Routzahn and Queen Victoria Spencer. They have done much to popularise the best British novelties in the United States.

Bush.—The Bush Sweet Peas are a section growing about two feet high, which originated in America. They will grow without sticks, but are the better for short supports. They are suitable for mixed borders, and also for pot culture, but are not in much demand for British gardens. Seed can be bought in separate colours or in mixture from a few of the largest seedsmen.

California.—See "America" and "Morse."

Carter.—The firm of James Carter & Co., of High Holborn, London, was closely identified with the early stages of Sweet Pea development. They introduced the famous Blue-edged, which was the first Picotee-edged variety, also Invincible Scarlet, Invincible Striped and Violet Queen. They have extensive trials of Sweet Peas at the present day.

Catalogues.—Sweet Pea lovers find the catalogues of the principal firms full of interest, containing, as they do, particulars of the leading varieties and novelties; also, in many cases, coloured plates and photographic illustrations. As a rule, the number of seeds is quoted with the price of the packets. A catalogue of varieties, giving the colours and raisers, is given in an Appendix to this work.

Christy, E. H.—An amateur grower of Sweet Peas at Ingatestone, Essex. Served on the Floral Committee of the National Sweet Pea Society.

Clarke, Major Trevor.—Raiser of the famous old Sweet Pea Blue-edged. See "Carter."

Classification.—The National Sweet Pea Society classifies Sweet Peas according to colour. The system was first proposed by the present author. Every year the Society publishes in its Annual what it considers to be the best varieties under the following colours: White, Crimson and Scarlet, Rose and Carmine, Yellow and Buff, Blue, Blush, Cerise, Pink, Orange shades, Lavender. Violet and Purple, Magenta, Picotee-edged, Fancy, Mauve, Maroon and Bronze, Striped and Flaked Purple and Blue, Striped and Flaked Red and Rose, Bicolor, Cream Pink, Marbled. The list is a useful guide to amateurs.

Clumps.—The cultivation of Sweet Peas in clumps is very popular. Clumps look well in herbaceous borders, on lawns, and near Rose Pillars. If the stations are well-prepared and the clumps are fairly large, a splendid effect is produced. A clump is best formed by planting in a circle, which should not be less than a yard across, and is better two. The plants should not be nearer than six inches apart. See Chapter VII.

Cole, Silas.—Head gardener to Earl Spencer, Althorp Park, Northampton. The first waved Sweet Pea, Countess Spencer, was exhibited by Mr. Cole in 1900, at Shrewsbury; and it was shown by him in London the following year, where it received a first-class certificate. This famous variety marked a new epoch in Sweet Pea history. Its origin has excited much controversy. The general belief is that it came as a sport in the plain standard pink Prima Donna, and this is strengthened by the fact that a somewhat similar sport, Gladys Unwin, came in Prima Donna on the grounds of Mr. W. J. Unwin, at Histon, near Cambridge. A similar variety also came on Mr. Eckford's grounds at Wem, Shropshire. All three appeared about the same time. A writer who is understood to have received special information from Mr. Cole has given the following as the origin of Countess Spencer: The varieties Triumph and Lovely were crossed. An unfixed seedling which resulted was crossed with Prima Donna. The waved pink resulting from this second cross was Countess Spencer. The stock of seed was acquired by Mr. Robert Sydenham and sent to California to be grown. The progeny proved to be unfixed, and many different colours appeared in it. These were attributed to the accidental intermixture with Countess Spencer of a few ripe seed pods from a cross made in 1900 between Countess Spencer and Salopian. Amongst the varieties thus produced was the rich carmine John Ingman. I have, however, been personally told by Mr. Cole that Lord Rosebery was one of the parents of John Ingman, and it is a well-known fact that the former appeared in John Ingman after the latter was placed on the market. An orange "rogue" also appeared in the Althorp Countess Spencer, and was named Hon. Mrs. C. R. Spencer; but as the waved orange was first shown to the National Sweet Pea Society as Helen Lewis by Mr. J. Watson, Jun., that name was accepted for it. Mr. Eckford's and Mr. Unwin's waved pinks came true. Whatever opinions may be held as to the exact origin of Countess Spencer it is accepted by every expert that Prima Donna was one of its parents. The latter was noted for its good habit of producing four flowers on a stem, a character common to the waved or Spencer Sweet Peas. The waved salmon Earl Spencer and the waved maroon Silas Cole also originated at Althorp Park, in addition to other varieties. See also fertilisation.

Colonies.—Sweet Peas have become very popular in all the British Colonies. An interesting article on Sweet Peas in New Zealand appeared in the National Sweet Pea Society's Annual for 1909. See also Chapter XVII.

Colours.—There is a considerable range of colours in Sweet Peas, as will be seen by reference to "Classification." A deep, bright yellow is the principal want (see Appendix for varieties which most nearly approach this colour). Some of the colours are difficult to describe, and the French Colour Chart issued at a reduced price by the Royal Horticultural Society, Vincent Square, Westminster, will be found very useful by those who wish to compare and describe colours. The task of blending and contrasting colours in the flower garden is interesting. Salmon and violet blue, cream and mauve, crimson and white, pale blue and white, pale blue and cream, salmon, pink and yellow, salmon pink and lavender, red, white and blue, all look well together. See also Chapter VII.

Commelin, Caspar.—A Dutch botanist to whom Franciscus Cupani (see "Cupani") sent seeds of Sweet Peas. See *Historical Notes* by Mr. S. B. Dicks in the National Sweet Pea Society's Annual for 1908.

Cross-fertilisation. See Fertilisation.

Cupani.—Franciscus Cupani was an Italian monk, who first sent the Sweet Pea to England, from Sicily, in 1699. The recipient was Dr. Uvedale, of Enfield. See Chapter II.

Cupid.—The section of Sweet Peas known as Cupids originated in California. The first, a white, appeared with Messrs. C. C. Morse & Co. in 1893, and it was exhibited in London in 1895, when the Royal Horticultural Society gave it an Award of Merit. Other colours appeared, and primrose, pink and white, apple-blossom, rose, red-striped, scarlet, blue and maroon can be had from the large seedsmen. The Cupids only grow a few inches high, and although they produce small tendrils, they do not climb. They are best suited for pot-culture and for edgings. They have the peculiarity of casting their buds, and this militates against them. I had considerable success with them once on a low bank containing a good deal of limestone, and partly shaded by large trees. They cast a few of their buds, but sufficient flowers opened to insure the beauty of the plants.

Curtis, Charles H.—Of Adelaide Road, Brentford, Middlesex, second secretary of the National Sweet Pea Society, part Editor of its Annual, and a notable writer on the flower. In 1908, a handsome testimonial, with a purse of gold, was presented to Mr. Curtis by the National Sweet

Pea Society for the valuable services which he had rendered to it.

Cuthbertson, William.—President of the National Sweet Pea Society, in 1908. Head of the firm of Dobbie & Co., florists and seedsmen. A valuable paper by Mr. Cuthbertson on *Mendelism as applied to Sweet Peas* was published in the National Sweet Pea Society's Annual for 1909.

Cutting-back.—See "Stopping."

Cuttings.—The Sweet Pea is one of the few Annuals which can be propagated by cuttings. See Chapter IV.

Daniels Bros.—Seedsmen at Norwich. Large growers of Sweet Peas.

Darlington, T. W.—Sweet Pea specialist at Warton, Carnforth. Introducer of Miss A. Brown.

Deal, William.—A seed grower at Kelvedon, Essex, who has devoted special study to Sweet Peas. Raiser of the varieties Winsome, Queenie, Colleen, Bertrand Deal, Winifred Deal and Giant Cream Waved, amongst others.

Decoration.—See "Rooms."

Dicks, S. B.—Served on the Floral Committee of the National Sweet Pea Society. Has travelled widely and devoted close study to Sweet Pea history. See *Historical Notes* in the National Sweet Pea Society's Annual for 1908, where some interesting illustrations of the first Sweet Peas grown in England are given; and *American Notes* in the Annual for 1909.

Dickson, Alex., & Sons.—Of Royal Avenue, Belfast, and Newtownards. These famous rosarians are very large growers of Sweet Peas.

Digges, H. J. R.—Of Donnybrook, Dublin. An Irish amateur grower and exhibitor. One of the first to encourage the culture of Sweet Peas in Ireland.

Dipnall, T. H.—Of Bourne, Lincolnshire. A writer on and raiser of Sweet Peas. See the National Sweet Pea Society's Annual for 1909 for a clever paper on Sweet Pea names; also Chapter III. of this work.

Diseases.—The Sweet Pea is subject to several diseases, particulars of which, with methods of prevention, are given in Chapter XI.

Dobbie & Co.—Florists and seedsmen, of Edinburgh, and Mark's Tey, Essex. Large growers of Sweet Peas, and introducers of several beautiful varieties, notably Edrom Beauty (see also " Simpson " and " Malcolm "), Masterpiece (see also " Malcolm "), Mrs. Hugh Dickson, Menie Christie, Hannah Dale and Princess Victoria.

Double.—Sweet Peas with two standards and extra wings are not uncommon, and these may be called double Sweet Peas. They are not specially desirable.

Drayson, G. F.—A well-known writer on Sweet Peas living at South Woodford, Essex. See the National Sweet Pea Society's Annual for 1909.

Duncan, Thomas.—A remarkably successful Scottish amateur grower of Sweet Peas. Head teacher of the village school at Fogo, near Duns. Mr. Duncan has won prizes in the principal competitions, showing flowers of grand quality.

Eckford, Henry, V.M.H.—The "father" of the modern Sweet Pea, and the founder of the Sweet Pea industry. Henry Eckford was a Scotsman by birth, and while serving as head gardener to families in England, he commenced crossing Sweet Peas. Extraordinary success attended his efforts. He raised the majority of the most popular varieties prior to the Countess Spencer era, such as Lord Rosebery, Dorothy Tennant, Dorothy Eckford, Mrs. Walter Wright, Mrs. Eckford, Henry Eckford, Captain of the Blues, Lady Grizel Hamilton, Miss Willmott, Lady Mary Currie, Prima Donna (parent of Countess Spencer), Prince of Wales, Scarlet Gem, Queen Alexandra, King Edward VII. and Romola Piazzani. Henry Eckford died at a ripe old age. See also Chapter III.

Enemies.—The Sweet Pea has several dangerous insect and fungoid enemies. For particulars and methods of prevention see Chapter XI.

Engelmann, G.—A grower of Sweet Peas at Saffron Walden, who has developed a strain of Winter-blooming varieties. Mr. Engelmann exhibited blooms before the National Sweet Pea Society in 1906. See Chapter X.

Essex.—This county contains the largest area of Sweet Peas in the United Kingdom. Immense quantities are grown for seed, principally at or near Coggeshall, Kelvedon, Feering, Witham and Mark's Tey. The fields of Sweet Peas form a picture of remarkable beauty in July. See an article on the Essex seed farms in the National Sweet Pea Society's Annual for 1909 by Mr. E. W. King.

Everlasting Pea.—The Everlasting Pea, *Lathyrus latifolius* of the older botanists, is a perennial. There are many beautiful varieties, but the flowers are not fragrant. Many attempts have been made to cross the Sweet Pea with the Everlasting Pea, but they have proved abortive. The most desirable result likely to attend successful cross-fertilisation is increasing the number of flowers of the Sweet Pea.

Exhibitions.—Shows of Sweet Peas have become regular functions since the formation of the National Sweet Pea and minor societies. No kind of flower makes a more beautiful exhibition than the Sweet Pea. The shows of the National Sweet Pea Society are generally held in the hall of the Royal Horticultural Society, Vincent Square, Westminster, London, in July, when the principal growers compete. The following are the principal points for exhibitors :—

Form of flower: The standard must be erect, waved or only slightly hooded. The standard, wings and keel should be well balanced. A small standard with large, irregular wings, or partially expanded keel, is defective. *Colour:* The colours should be clear, fresh and bright. Selfs are preferred to stripes and flakes. *Number of flowers:* There should be at least three flowers on a stem, preferably four, and they should be neatly disposed, not scattered over a long extent of stem. *Number and length of stems:* There should be about twenty stems, lightly arranged in each vase. Fifteen to eighteen inches is a good length of stem. A little heather or moss may be used in the mouth of the vase to fix the stems. *Foliage:* It is not desirable to use foliage; if any is used it should be Sweet Pea leafage, or flower sprays of *Gypsophila paniculata*. *Gathering:* The flowers are best gathered while quite dry, with the full length of stalk (fig 12) and with only two flowers open at the most. They are best gathered the day before the show. The stems should be placed in water at once and put in a cool, shady building. *Packing:* The flowers should be removed from the water and packed perfectly dry and firm in soft paper. Directly the show ground is reached the stems should be placed in water again. *Judging:* The Royal Horticultural Society suggests judging on a maximum of six points for each variety, divided as follows :— Form and substance, 2; colour and freshness, 2; attractive setting up, 2. *Duplicates:* If the schedule specifies distinct varieties take care to avoid putting in duplicates. This mistake is easily made if the competitor is pressed for time, or has the same variety under different names. Exhibitors should refer to the Too-much-alike list of the National Sweet Pea Society. (See Appendix.) For fuller remarks on exhibitions and exhibition culture see Chapters V. and VIII.

Fertilisation.—The Sweet Pea is a hermaphrodite flower, the two sexes being united in the same bloom. It is the

Fig. 12.—A SPRAY AT THE RIGHT STAGE TO GATHER FOR PACKING.
Note how the finger and thumb are placed to pluck it.

rule for it to be self-fertilised, as the stigma is receptive and the pollen ripe while the flower is still in the bud stage, or insufficiently opened to permit of cross-fertilisation by the wind or insect agency. It is because of this that the varieties multiplied very slowly in past years. If a florist wishes to cross-fertilise he must prevent the flower on which he proposes to operate from being self-fertilised with its own pollen by opening it in its undeveloped stage and removing the anthers before the pollen has become loose; he can then apply pollen from another flower which he has selected as a parent. The modern waved or Spencer type of Sweet Pea has a more open keel than the old type, and the stigma has been known to protrude before it has become receptive. In such cases natural cross-fertilisation is possible, as the pollen of the abnormal flower may fall back into the keel instead of being blown on to the stigma, and pollen from another flower may be carried to the exposed receptive stigma by the wind. It should be noted that there is often loose pollen about expanded flowers. Nevertheless, natural cross-fertilisation remains the exception. See also Chapter III.

Fixing.—This term is applied to the establishment of the characters of a new variety. When a cross is effected and seed saved, the progeny resulting may be various. One may be selected as desirable, and seed saved from that alone. The next year the plants may not all come true, and those differing in colour are termed "rogues." The removal of rogues must be persisted in until no more appear, when the variety is fixed. Modern Sweet Peas have proved difficult to fix, doubtless because unfixed varieties were used as parents. If the parents themselves are not fixed there is sure to be trouble in fixing the offspring. The seed of each individual plant should be gathered and sown separately. A study of Mendel's laws is useful to raisers. See also Chapter III.

Floral Committee.—The Floral Committee of the National Sweet Pea Society consists of thirteen members, seven of whom are amateurs and six tradesmen. The Chairman must be an amateur. The duty of the Committee is to report on the trials of the Society, and to draw up the Classification and Too-much-alike lists, annually.

Foster, Charles.—While Assistant Director and Horticultural Instructor at Reading University, Mr. Charles Foster had charge of the trials of the National Sweet Pea Society. An excellent cultivator and earnest student of Sweet Peas, Mr. Foster did valuable service.

Gathering.—See note under exhibitions, also Chapter VIII.

Germination.—Complaints of the bad germination of Sweet Peas are common every Winter and Spring. The lavender and mauve varieties, most of which have small, wrinkled seeds, cause the most disappointments. A common cause of bad germination is excessive watering. The soil should be very sandy, and only sufficient water should be given to prevent the soil becoming dust dry. Close, wet soil is bad. Very hard seed that is slow to germinate may be stimulated by soaking it in water and then peeling off the hard skin. See also " seed."

Gilbert & Son.—Seed growers and florists at Dyke, Bourne, Lincolnshire, specialists in Anemones and Sweet Peas. Amongst other varieties of the latter raised by Messrs. Gilbert & Son may be named Albert Gilbert, Countess of Ancaster, Cherry Ripe, Miss Frills, Mrs. Wilcox (a waved America), and Sunrise.

Hemus, Miss Hilda.—Sweet Pea specialist at Holdfast Hall, Upton-on-Severn, Worcestershire. Miss Hemus first came into prominence with the beautiful Picotee-edged, cream-ground variety Evelyn Hemus. She has introduced a large number of beautiful varieties, including Zephyr (with Mr. W. J. Unwin), Zero, Zara, Zarina, Lucy Hemus, Paradise Ivory, Holdfast Belle, Paradise Red Flake, Charles Hemus, Paradise Apple Blossom, Helio Paradise, Zebra and Coccinea Paradise.

Herbert, George.—Of Sutton Scotney, Hampshire. Served on the Floral Committee of the National Sweet Pea Society. Raiser of new varieties.

History.—For the history of the Sweet Pea see Chapter II.

Hitchins, Martin F.—Of Trevarrick, St. Austell, Cornwall. A well-known amateur grower of Sweet Peas. Served on the Floral Committee of the National Sweet Pea Society.

Holmes, R.—A seed grower at Tuckswood, Norwich, specialising Sweet Peas. Raiser of Herbert Smith, a sunproof crimson, and other varieties.

Hooded.—A Sweet Pea is spoken of as a hooded variety when the standard folds over towards the wings. Lady Grizel Hamilton is a typical hooded variety.

House, Isaac & Son.—Florists and seedsmen at Westbury-on-Trym, near Bristol. Specialists in Sweet Peas and successful exhibitors. Raisers of Lord Nelson, Yankee, Harold, and other varieties.

Hurst & Son.—Large wholesale seed growers and merchants at Feering, Essex, and Houndsditch, London. Introducers of St. George and other varieties.

Hutchins, Rev. W. T.—A famous American writer on Sweet Peas, author of the famous phrase: "The Sweet Pea has a keel that was meant to seek all shores; it has wings that were meant to fly across all Continents; it has a standard which is friendly to all nations, and it has a fragrance like the universal Gospel, yea, a sweet prophecy of welcome everywhere that has been abundantly fulfilled."

Insects.—Several insects are inimical to the Sweet Pea. For description and methods of extirpation see Chapter XI. A very small black beetle (*Meligethes*) crawls about the flowers, but it is harmless. It has been suspected of causing cross-fertilisation by carrying pollen from flower to flower, but this must be rare, as I have never found it in the buds, and self-fertilisation usually takes place before the buds open.

Introduction.—The Sweet Pea was first sent to England from Sicily in 1699, by Franciscus Cupani. See "Cupani" and Chapter II.

Ireland, Andrew.—A raiser of Sweet Peas at Mark's Tey, Essex. Served on the Floral Committee of the National Sweet Pea Society. One of the most expert growers of Sweet Peas.

Jones, H. J.—A florist and seedsman at Lewisham, London, and Keston, Kent. Specialist in Sweet Peas. Raiser of Mrs. Chic Holmes, Keston Red, and other varieties.

Jones, J.—A raiser of Sweet Peas at Wem, Shropshire. Served on the Floral Committee of the National Sweet Pea Society.

Jones, Thomas.—A famous amateur grower of Sweet Peas at Bryn Pen-y-lan, near Ruabon, North Wales. A successful exhibitor at nearly all the principal shows. Served on the Floral Committee of the National Sweet Pea Society.

Judging.—For hints on judging Sweet Peas see "Exhibitions."

King, E. W., & Co.—Seed growers at Coggeshall, Essex. Specialists in Sweet Peas. Introducers of Phœnix, Anglian Blue and other varieties. See an article on the Essex seed farms by Mr. E. W. King in the National Sweet Pea Society's Annual for 1909.

King, J. K., & Co.—Old established and extensive seed growers at Coggeshall, Essex. Large cultivators of Sweet Peas.

Lathyrus.—The Sweet Pea is *Lathyrus odoratus* of Linnæus. *Lathyrus* comes from *la*, to add to; and *thouros*, an irritant; as the seeds are suposed to have the quality of increasing excitement. The natural order is Leguminosæ.

Laxton, Thomas.—A famous specialist in cross-fertilisation. His principal work was with culinary Peas, but he also worked on Sweet Peas, raising Invincible Blue, Invincible Carmine, and other varieties.

Leak, G. W.—A raiser and grower of Sweet Peas at Wisbech, Cambridgeshire. Author of an interesting article, with a proposed new Colour Classification, in the National Sweet Pea Society's Annual for 1909.

Lumley, Wm.—Sweet Pea specialist at Havant, Hampshire. Introducer of Anna Lumley, Constance Oliver, Marjorie Willis, and other varieties.

Mackereth, H. W.—Sweet Pea specialist at Ulverston, Lancashire, devoting particular attention to the cultivation and distribution of novelties. Manufacturer of a special Sweet Pea Manure.

Malcolm, Alex.—Amateur specialist of Sweet Peas at Duns, Scotland. A successful exhibitor at all the principal shows. Has remarkable clumps, often growing to twelve feet high, and supported by wire frames. Raiser of Masterpiece, Mrs. Malcolm, Malcolm's Waved Cream, and other varieties. Served on the Floral Committee of the National Sweet Pea Society.

Manures.—The subject of manures is one of great importance to the Sweet Pea grower, and particularly to the exhibitor. It is generally agreed that rich, decayed yard manure is the best, but artificials are very useful. See "Artificial Manures," also Chapter V.

Market.—Sweet Peas are extremely extensively grown for market, but the culture is not so remunerative as it used to be, the prices being lower. For full particulars see Chapter IX.

Mendel.—Gregor Johann Mendel, Abbot of Brunn, born 1822, died 1884, propounded certain principles of heredity in relation to cross-fertilisation which have engaged the earnest attention of Sweet Pea raisers. See Chapter III., also the National Sweet Pea Society's Annual for 1909, where an article on Mendelism by Mr. Wm. Cuthbertson appears. For fuller information see "Mendel's Principles of Heredity," by W. Bateson, Cambridge University Press; and "Mendelism," by R. C. Punnett (Bowes & Bowes, Cambridge).

Miller, S.—Sweet Pea grower of Newport, Isle of Wight. Raiser of Ivy Miller, Magnificent, and other sorts.

Morse, C. C., & Co.—Sweet Pea growers and merchants at San Francisco, California. Raisers of Helen Pierce, Florence Morse Spencer, Flora Norton Spencer, Asta Ohn, and many other varieties. Introducers of the Cupid Sweet Peas. Associated with Messrs. W. Atlee Burpee & Co. (see "Burpee") in the introduction of many famous varieties.

National Sweet Pea Society.—A development of the Sweet Pea Bicentenary Committee of 1900, the National Sweet Pea Society has grown into a powerful organisation, with a large membership, a Floral Committee, a series of trials, and an Annual containing articles by experts. The Society holds a show in London every year, generally at the Royal Horticultural Society's Hall in Vincent Square, Westminster, and another show at a selected place in the provinces. It considers the home grower, however, as well as the exhibitor, and disseminates much valuable information for his guidance. The publication of a Classification List of the best varieties, and of a Too-much-alike List, adds greatly to the benefits conferred by the society on its members. The annual subscription is five shillings. The first secretary of the Society was Mr. Horace J. Wright, of Dault Road, Wandsworth, London; and the second Mr. Charles H. Curtis, of Adelaide Road, Brentford, Middlesex.

Nitro-Bacterine.—This is a commercial culture of *Pseudomonas radicicola*, the beneficent bacterium which causes the nodules on the roots of Sweet Peas by fixing free atmospheric nitrogen. Many experimentalists have failed to observe any good results from its use on Sweet Peas, but certain successes have been recorded. It may be expected to show better results in poor than in rich soil. For the results of experiments on Peas with Nitro-bacterine see the Journal of the Royal Horticultural Society for November, 1908.

Packing.—The packing of flowers in cotton wool is an old fault. It is particularly bad for Sweet Peas, which are best without any material other than soft paper. They should be gathered while dry, with some of the flowers on each stem still in the bud stage; and they should be packed firmly. See "Exhibitions," also Chapters VIII. and IX.

Planting.—Sweet Peas raised under glass are best planted, as a rule, in April. The exact period should depend on the state of the soil and the weather. The ground is in the best condition when moist (but not sodden) and crumbly. Disturbance of the roots should be avoided as much as possible. See Chapter VI.

Plukenet.—Leonard Plukenet, born in 1642, had a botanic garden at Westminster, and established an Herbarium, which now forms a part of the Hans Sloane Collection at the Natural History Museum, South Kensington. The Herbarium contains buds, flowers and leaves of what Mr. S. B. Dicks considers to be the oldest specimen of Sweet Peas in existence. See the National Sweet Pea's Society's Annual for 1908.

Pot Culture.—The Sweet Pea is not ill-adapted for pot-culture. See Chapter X.

Properties.—Like other florists' flowers, the Sweet Pea has been given certain defined Properties for the guidance of raisers, exhibitors and judges. See "Exhibitions."

Reading.—The trials of the National Sweet Pea Society were conducted in the gardens of University College, Reading, for several years. Near London, and enjoying an excellent service of fast trains, Reading proved to be a convenient centre. The extensive trials of the great seed firm of Sutton & Sons formed a powerful additional attraction for visitors.

Rogues.—In the early years of a new variety, flowers of a different colour or form appear in it; these are termed "rogues," and have to be eliminated by careful selection. On the thoroughness with which "rogueing" is done the purity of a stock turns. Much of the want of purity of American stocks is attributed to the difficulty of thorough rogueing, which arises from the plants being grown in California without supports. When grown on sticks or wire it is easier to get the bad plant out, but even then care should be taken to follow the rogue right to the root. Sometimes a "rogue" is distinct, and good in itself; in such cases the seed should be saved from it and sown separately. It should be given a number and an entry in the trial book. See Chapter III.

Rooms.—Sweet Peas are charming flowers for room decoration. They are light, graceful, with beautiful colours and delicious perfume. Pink, rose, scarlet and white look best by artificial light. The blues and mauves, though charming by daylight, are ineffectual at night. As a rule, Sweet Peas should not be mixed with other flowers, but the gauzy flower-sprays of Gypsophila paniculata may be mingled with them, taking the place of foliage. No leafage other than Sweet Peas should be used as a rule, but where the flowers are associated with Roses, Rose foliage may be used. Pale pink Sweet Peas look charming in a wide bowl with the deep pink Rose, Dorothy Perkins, and long shoots of the latter with their glossy green leaves add to the effect. Pink Sweet Peas also mix well with the long, Gladiolus-like flower stems of the popular annuals, Godetia Dwarf Rose and Clarkia elegans flore pleno. Care should be taken in mixing Sweet Peas of various colours. See hints under "Colour." It is an advantage to have long stems, and those come with good culture. If fully expanded flowers are gathered they should be picked in the evening or early morning, but stems with only a portion of the flowers open may be gathered while dry, and will develop in water. It is not easy to arrange Sweet Peas lightly in vases, and the best way is to hold the bunch of flowers in the hand, let the ends of the stems drop on the table, and then, holding them over the vase, set the stems in the vases with a little moss. The fall causes the flowers to separate, and those on long stems stand above those on shorter ones.

Rothera, T., & Co.—Nurserymen at Burton Joyce, Notts. Raisers of Mrs. Rothera, which was subsequently named Queen by Messrs. Sutton & Sons, who purchased the stock.

Rows.—Sweet Peas are generally grown in rows, and if these run north and south the sun gets full play on both sides. The distance apart of the rows should vary with the vigour of the plants, but should rarely be less than six feet. One row may consist of several varieties in larger or shorter blocks. A pound of Sweet Pea seed will sow about 120 yards of row.

Saving.—When Sweet Peas of any value are being saved the pods should be gathered separately; it would not do to trust to pulling and thrashing. The pods are ready when they have lost their fresh colour and begin to shrivel. They should be stored in a cool, dry place until selling or sowing time. In dealing with unfixed novelties it is wise to keep the pods of each plant separate, as this facilitates fixing.

Scent.—It is satisfactory to know that improvements in the size, form and colour of Sweet Peas have not been obtained at the cost of scent. The perfume of the Sweet Pea is one of its greatest charms, and any development which entailed loss of odour should be discouraged.

Seeds.—The seeds of Sweet Peas are borne in pods, the number in each pod varying from eight to twelve. The seeds of most varieties are smooth and round, but the blues and lavenders have small, wrinkled, insignificant seeds as a rule, and beginners often have grave misgivings as to their freshness. The Sweet Pea seed industry is of gigantic proportions. More than one retail firm in Great Britain distributes several tons annually, and as the seed is made up in small packets containing from six to fifty seeds each, the number of buyers must extend to hundreds of thousands. A pound of Sweet Pea seeds contains from 5,000 to 10,000. John Ingman contains about 5,000; Helen Pierce 6,400; Countess Spencer and Miss Willmott 5,500 each; Lady Grizel Hamilton 7,000; and Frank Dolby 9,500. The distribution of Sweet Peas in collections, the varieties composing which are specified by the dealer, is very popular. Most of the white-flowered varieties have light-coloured seeds, but there is an interesting exception in Sadie Burpee, one stock of which has black seeds. Two ounces per yard run of row is a fair quantity of seed of the Spencers, and six to eight ounces of the old type. An ingenious instrument for counting Sweet Pea seeds, put on the market by Messrs. Blake & Mackenzie, is used by many seedsmen. See also " saving " and Chapter IV.

Self-fertilisation.—Owing to the fact that the organs of the Sweet Pea are mature while the flower is nearly or quite closed, the flowers are normally self-fertilised, or " selfed," to use the florists' phrase. See " Fertilisation."

Shade.—The early scarlet and crimson Sweet Peas had not substance enough to stand the sun, and lost their colour, but modern varieties are sunproof; and it is practically only the salmons that " burn." These may be placed in positions where they receive shade from trees or buildings in the hottest parts of the day. If exposed, artificial shade should be provided. Tiffany, a light, inexpensive canvas which seedsmen sell, answers well if fixed on a frame above the flowers. In the soft light which filters through it the colours shine with a beautiful glow.

Showing.—See "Exhibitions."

Simpson, Rev. Macduff.—An amateur grower at Edrom Manse, Duns, N.B. Raiser (with Mr. Alex. Malcolm) of Edrom Beauty.

Smith, Fletcher, & Co.—Iron and wirework manufacturers at High Street, Edinburgh, who have devised improved forms of Sweet Pea supports and trainers, notably a collapsible wire trainer.

Smith, Herbert.—Of R. Sydenham, Limited, Tenby Street, Birmingham. Trade dealer. Served on the Floral Committee of the National Sweet Pea Society.

Societies.—The number of societies devoted to the Sweet Pea is growing rapidly, and they do much good in bringing lovers of the flower together and holding exhibitions. The National Sweet Pea Society is the leading organisation, and its rules afford a useful guide to minor societies. See "National Sweet Pea Society."

Soil.—The Sweet Pea thrives on almost all soils when the ground is well prepared. Deep cultivation, thorough disintegration and liberal manuring are the three principal essentials. See Chapter V.

Sowing.—Success in Sweet Pea culture turns considerably on the sowing. Those who sow in pots or boxes should guard against keeping the soil wet. It should be moist, but not saturated. See Chapter IV.

Spencer.—The Sweet Peas with waved standards are commonly spoken of as "Spencers," owing to the fact that Countess Spencer was the first variety of this character. See "Cole."

Sports.—A seminal variation sometimes occurs in the Sweet Pea, and is termed a "sport." Owing to its provision for self-fertilisation (see "Fertilisation") sporting is not so common in the Sweet Pea as in many other florists' flowers, but it has been more common since the advent of the Countess Spencer class. If the variation has no special distinctiveness and beauty it is treated as a rogue and thrown away; if it is distinct and good the seed is saved from it and sown separately the following year. With persistent rogueing it is eventually fixed. Amateurs who have not the opportunity of visiting extensive trials of Sweet Peas and shows, are often in doubt as to the value of any variation which they may have. Their best course is to submit it to an expert, and this can always be done through the horticultural papers. When they have got it fixed, and have secured a stock of seed, the variety should be sent to the National Sweet Pea Society for trial. If distinct and good it will receive an award, and it has then a real pecuniary value; offers for the stock of seed will come freely from the seedsmen.

Stark, G., & Son.—Seed growers at Great Ryburgh, Norfolk. Specialists in Sweet Peas, and raisers of many good varieties, including Florence Wright, Mercia, Mrs. Duncan, Elegance, Silver Wings, Olive Ruffell, Winnie Jones, Mrs. R. W. Pitt and Lady Farren.

Stevenson, Thomas.—Head Gardener at Woburn Place, Addlestone, Surrey. A famous grower of Sweet Peas and a highly successful competitor at the principal shows. Served on the Floral Committee of the National Sweet Pea Society. Raiser of Rosie Adams and other varieties.

Sticks.—Although wire is now used a good deal for supporting Sweet Peas the majority of growers retain sticks. They may consist of Larch, Hazel, Ash or Chestnut, and will cost fourpence to sixpence per bundle of twenty five. One bundle will do four yards of row well, allowing for both sides. The sticks should be fresh and tall. The base should be sharpened to facilitate forcing in. The sticks should be placed in position while the plants are quite young.

Stopping.—It is not an uncommon practice to stop Sweet Peas. Some growers stop their plants at a foot high to encourage side shoots from the base, others let half go to four feet and the remainder to six feet before stopping. The effect of stopping is to encourage late flowers on side growths. so insuring a succession of good flowers. Early plants that have flowered may be cut back close to the ground in July, and will often throw up fresh growth and produce fine late flowers.

Suburban Gardens.—Sweet Peas are well suited for suburban gardens, where they will cover walls and trellis work, and form clumps.

Sutton & Sons.—Seedsmen at Reading, Berkshire, where they have extensive trial grounds and warehouses. Large growers of Sweet Peas. Make a feature of fine selections of the principal colours, and also of colour blends. Introducers of Queen, Marbled Blue, and other varieties,

Sydenham, Robert.—Seedsman at Tenby Street, Birmingham, doing a very large trade in Sweet Peas. Makes a special feature of popular collections. Introducer of Herbert Smith and other varieties.

Télemly.—For information about Télemly Winter-flowering Sweet Peas see "Arkwright," and Chapter X.

Teschemacher, E.—An amateur grower at Chesham, Bucks. See the Sweet Pea Annual for 1909, where an article on Sweet Peas in pots by Mr. Teschemacher appears.

Thomas, Harry H.—An amateur grower at Hanwell, Middlesex, and a well-known writer on Sweet Peas.

Too-much-alike Varieties.—The National Sweet Pea Society publishes a list of varieties in its Annual every year, in which those sorts which are too much alike to be admissible in the same show stand are bracketted together. All growers, and exhibitors in particular, should study this list. See Appendix to this work.

Trials.—The trials of Sweet Peas conducted by the National Sweet Pea Society and the large seedsmen are both interesting and instructive. Amateur and trade growers alike should lose no opportunity of inspecting them, in order to keep up-to-date with sorts and to become acquainted with the best stocks.

Tubs.—Sweet Peas may be successfully grown in large tubs, and this method of culture is convenient for suburban gardeners whose borders and beds are very small. Good clumps in tubs look very nice, and the tubs can be shifted from place to place.

Unwin, W. J.—A famous raiser of Sweet Peas at Histon, Cambridge, enjoying a high reputation for the excellence of his stocks. Raiser of Gladys Unwin, Jack Unwin, Chrissie Unwin, Douglas Unwin, Mrs. W. J. Unwin, Mrs. E. F. Drayson, Rosabelle Hoare, Gladys French, Bobby K., Frank Dolby, E. J. Castle, and many other famous varieties. The waved pink Gladys Unwin came in Prima Donna with Mr. W. J. Unwin at the same time that Countess Spencer came with Mr. S. Cole at Althorp Park, Northampton.

Varieties.—There is a very large number of varieties of Sweet Peas. See Chapter XII., also Appendix.

Vases.—Sweet Peas are charming flowers for vase decoration. (See "Rooms.") Vases of various kinds are used for setting up flowers at shows. (See "Exhibitions".) One of the best is Mr. Thomas Jones's patent vase, which is supplied by Sweet Pea dealers.

Ward, H. E.—An amateur grower at Vicar's Cross, Chester. Has raised Spencer or Waved Varieties from Old-type sorts by crossing Scarlet Gem with an unfixed seedling from a Miss Willmott-Gorgeous cross. A writer on Sweet Peas.

Ward, Sidney.—A trade grower at Stratford, New Zealand. Hon. Secretary to the Stratford (N.Z.) Horticultural Society. See the National Sweet Pea Society's Annual for 1909, where an article by Mr. Ward on "Sweet Peas in New Zealand" appears.

Watkins & Simpson.—Wholesale seed dealers at Tavistock Street, Covent Garden, London. Specialists in Sweet Peas. Introducers of Frank Dolby, Mrs. Alfred Watkins, Picotee, King Edward VII., Improved, Miss Willmott Improved, Gipsy Queen, and other varieties and selections. Conduct large trials on their grounds at Twickenham and Hounslow every year.

Watson, J., Jun.—A gardener at Kingston-on-Thames. Raiser of Helen Lewis. Served on the Floral Committee of the National Sweet Pea Society.

Waved.—For notes on the origin of the Waved or Spencer Sweet Pea see "Cole."

Webb and Sons.—Seedsmen at Wordsley, Stourbridge. Large growers and Exhibitors of Sweet Peas.

Winter-flowering Varieties.—For notes on Winter-flowering sections of Sweet Peas see "Arkwright," "Engelmann" and "Zvolanek," and Chapter X.

Wright, Horace J.—A trade dealer at Dault Road, Wandsworth, London. First Secretary of the National Sweet Pea Society and part Editor of its Annual. Introducer of Rosie Adams. A well-known writer on and judge of Sweet Peas.

Wright, Walter P.—Served as Chairman of the Floral Committee of the National Sweet Pea Society. Author of the present and many other works on Gardening.

Zvolanek, A.—A market grower at Bound Brook, New Jersey, U.S.A., who has developed a Winter-flowering strain of Sweet Peas that is very popular in America.

APPENDIX.

A CATALOGUE OF VARIETIES OF SWEET PEAS, WITH SELECTIONS.

STUDENTS of Sweet Peas like to have a record of existing varieties, to which reference can be made when necessary. Apart from its general interest, a list containing the names and descriptions of every known sort has particular value. It is helpful to raisers and introducers of new varieties, because it tells them what colours exist. It also enables them to avoid the duplication of names. The following is a descriptive list of Sweet Peas :—

NAME.	RAISER, INTRODUCER.	COLOUR OF STANDARD.	COLOUR OF WINGS.	PLAIN OR WAVED.
A. B. Bantock	Bakers	amber, buff and pink	buff	waved
Acme	H. J. Jones	faint blush	faint blush	plain
Admiral Togo	Breadmore	violet maroon	violet maroon	plain
Admiration	Morse, Burpee	rosy lavender	rosy lavender	plain
Adonis	Carter	carmine pink	pink	plain
Agnes Eckford	Eckford	pink	pink	plain
Agnes Johnston	Eckford	pink, shaded cream	pink shaded cream	slightly waved
A. J. Cook	Unwin, Watkins	purplish lavender	purplish lavender	plain
Albatross	Dobbie & Co	white	white	waved
Albert Gilbert	Gilbert & Son	rosy pink	pink	plain
Alice Eckford	Eckford	cream	white	plain
Albion	Stark	ivory	ivory	plain
Alba magnifica	Henderson	white	white	waved
Althorp Gem	Cole	lilac	lilac	plain
America	Morse, Vaughan	white, crimson stripes	white, crimson stripes	plain
American Belle	Burpee	rose and white spotted	rose and white spotted	plain
American Queen	Morse, Burpee	salmon red	rose	plain
Amethyst	Aldersey	mauve	mauve	waved
Anglian blue	E. W. King & Co.	sky blue	sky blue	waved
Anglian Carmine	E. W. King & Co.	carmine	carmine	waved
Anglian Orange	E. W. King & Co.	salmon pink	salmon pink	waved
Anglian Pink	E. W. King & Co.	pink	pink	waved

APPENDIX. 143

NAME.	RAISER, INTRODUCER.	COLOUR OF STANDARD.	COLOUR OF WINGS.	PLAIN OR WAVED.
Anna Lumley	Lumley	maroon	maroon	waved
Annie B. Gilroy	Eckford	cerise	cerise	plain
Annie Stark	Stark	white, flushed pink	white, flushed pink	plain
Apple Blossom	Eckford	rose	blush	plain
Apple Blossom Spencer	Burpee	rose	blush	waved
Argosy	House	rosy lavender	rosy lavender	plain
Arthur Unwin	Unwin	rose	buff	waved
Asta Ohn	Morse	lilac, shaded rose	lilac, shaded rose	waved
Audrey Crier	Breadmore	salmon pink	salmon pink	waved
Aurora	Burpee	white, striped salmon	white, striped salmon	plain
Aurora Spencer	Burpee	white, striped salmon	white, striped salmon	waved
Azure Fairy	Bath	French grey, watered blue	grey	waved
Bakers' Scarlet	Bakers	scarlet	scarlet	waved
Bath's Crimson	Bath	crimson	crimson	plain
Beacon	R. Bolton	cerise	cream	plain
Beatrice Spencer	Morse	white, tinted pink	white, tinted pink	waved
Beauty	Bolton, Sharpe	blush	blush	waved
Beauty of Althorp	Cole	rosy lavender	rosy lavender	waved
Bertrand Deal	Wm. Deal	rosy mauve	rosy mauve	waved
Biddy Perkin	Perkin	rosy mauve	rosy mauve	waved
Blackbird	Bolton, Sharpe	very dark maroon	dark maroon	waved
Black Knight	Eckford	shining maroon	maroon	plain
Black Michael	Eckford	reddish maroon	reddish maroon	plain
Blanche Burpee	Eckford	white	white	plain
Blanche Ferry	Ferry	carmine rose	white, shaded pink	plain
Blue-edged (Blue Hybrid)	Clarke, Carter	white, blue edge	white, blue edge	plain
Blue Eyes	Lumley	veined blue	veined blue	plain
Blushing Beauty	Dobble & Co.	pink, suffused lilac	pink, suffused lilac	plain
Blush Queen	Dobble	blush	blush	slightly waved
Blush Spencer	Breadmore	blush	blush	waved
Blush Spencer	E. W. King & Co.	blush	blush	waved
Bob	H. J. Jones	deep red	red	waved

NAME.	RAISER, INTRODUCER.	COLOUR OF STANDARD.	COLOUR OF WINGS.	PLAIN OR WAVED.
Bobby K.	Chandler, Unwin	blush	blush	waved
Bolton's Blue	R. Bolton	blue	blue	plain
Bolton's Pink	R. Bolton	pink	pink	plain
Boreatton	Eckford	maroon	maroon	plain
Bride of Niagara	Vick	carmine rose	white	plain
Bridesmaid	Morse, Vaughan	carmine	rose	plain
Brilliant	Morse, Burpee	bright crimson	crimson	plain
Brilliant Blue (Lord Nelson)	Burpee	dark blue	dark blue	plain
Britannia	Dobbie	white, flaked crimson	white, flaked crimson	plain
Bronze King	Haage & Schmidt	coppery pink	white	plain
Bronze Prince	Eckford, Bull	rose, flushed scarlet	blush	plain
Burpee's White Spencer	Burpee	white	white	waved
Burpee's Primrose Spencer	Burpee	cream	cream	waved
Buttercup	Lumley	cream	cream	slightly waved
Butterfly	Sutton	white, shaded mauve	white, shaded mauve	plain
California	Lynch	pale pink	pale pink	plain
Californian Sunbeams	Morse	primrose	primrose	plain
Calypso	Eckford	magenta	magenta	plain
Cambridge stripe	Sutton	blue flake	blue flake	plain
Cannell's White	Cannell	white	white	plain
Caprice	Johnson	white, shaded pink	white, shaded pink	plain
Captain Clarke	Clarke, Sharpe	white, pencilled	white, pencilled	plain
Captain of the Blues	Eckford	purplish blue	blue	plain
,, ,, Spencer	Morse	purple	blue	waved
Captivation	Eckford	rosy purple	rosy purple	plain
Cardinal	Eckford	crimson	crimson	plain
Carmen Sylva	Laxton	claret	lilac	plain
Carmine Rose	see Princess Beatrice.			
Cecil Crier	Breadmore	rosy pink	rosy pink	waved
Celestial	Lorenz	light mauve	lavender	plain

APPENDIX. 145

NAME.	RAISER, INTRODUCER.	COLOUR OF STANDARD.	COLOUR OF WINGS.	PLAIN OR WAVED.
Ceres	see Mrs. Collier.			
Chamois	see Dora Breadmore.			
Chancellor	Eckford	orange pink	orange pink	plain
Charles Hemus	Hemus	wine colour	wine colour	waved
Cherry Ripe	Gilbert & Son	cerise	cerise	waved
Chilton	Clark	salmon pink	salmon pink	waved
Chrissie Unwin	Unwin	cerise	cerise	waved
Clara Curtis	R. Bolton, Sharpe	cream	cream	waved
Coccinea	Eckford	cerise	cerise	plain
Coccinea Paradise	Hemus	cerise	cerise	waved
Codsall Rose	Bakers	pink	pink	waved
Colleen	Wm. Deal	rose	white	waved
Colonist	Eckford	rosy lilac	rosy lilac	plain
Columbia	Hutchins	red, white and blue striped	striped	plain
Constance Oliver	Lumley	pink, cream ground	pink, cream ground	waved
Contrast	Bath	blue and purple, white edge	blue and purple, white edge	
Coquette	Eckford	primrose	primrose	waved
Coral Gem	Tuttle, Vaughan	coral pink	coral pink	plain
Coronet	Walker, Hutchins	white, striped orange	white, striped orange	plain
Cottage Maid	see Duchess of Sutherland.			
Countess of Aberdeen	Eckford	white, flushed pink	white	plain
Countess Cadogan	Eckford	violet	light blue	plain
Countess of Ancaster	Gilbert & Son	plum	plum	waved
Countess of Lathom	Eckford	pink	pink	plain
Countess of Northbrook	Breadmore	pale pink	pale pink	waved
Countess of Powis	Eckford	orange	pink	plain
Countess of Radnor	Eckford	pale mauve	lilac	plain
Countess of Shrewsbury	Eckford	pink, purple suffusion	pale lilac	plain
Countess Spencer	Cole	pink	pink	waved

146 A BOOK ABOUT SWEET PEAS.

NAME.	RAISER, INTRODUCER.	COLOUR OF STANDARD.	COLOUR OF WINGS.	PLAIN OR WAVED.
Cream of Brockhampton	Foster	cream	cream	plain
Cream Paradise	Hemus	cream	cream	waved
Creole	Morse, Burpee	pinkish lavender	lavender	plain
Crimson Paradise	Hemus	crimson	crimson	waved
Crown Jewel	Eckford	buff, rose tint	buff, rose tint	plain
Crown Princess of Prussia	Haage & Schmidt	pale pink	pale pink	plain
Cupid	Morse, Burpee	white	white	plain
Cyril Breadmore	Breadmore	rosy carmine	carmine	plain
Dainty	Morse, Burpee	white, pink edge	white, pink edge	plain
Dainty Spencer	Morse Burpee	picotee edge	picotee edge	waved
David R. Williamson	Eckford	indigo	blue	plain
Dawn	Stark	magenta	white, shaded crimson	plain
Daybreak	Hutchins, Burpee	white, marbled rose	white, marbled rose	plain
Dazzler	Breadmore	flame	flame	waved
Delicata	Breadmore	pink veined	pink veined	plain
Delight	Eckford	white, tipped crimson	white	plain
Devonshire Cream	Bathurst, Mackereth	cream	cream	plain
Distinction	Bath	white, red edge	white, red edge	waved
Dodwell F. Browne	Eckford	crimson	crimson	waved
Dolly Varden	Morse, Burpee	light purple	white, shaded purple	plain
Dora Breadmore	Breadmore	buff	buff	plain
Dora Cowper	see Mrs. Collier.			
Doris Cannell	Cannell	orange	rosy salmon	waved
Doris Clayton	Breadmore	lavender	lavender	waved
Doris Burt	Unwin	scarlet	scarlet	waved
Doris Stevenson	Stevenson	rosy lilac	lilac	waved
Dorothy Eckford	Eckford	white	white	plain
Dorothy Tennant	Eckford	mauve	mauve	plain
Dorothy Tigwell	Tigwell	scarlet	scarlet	plain
Dorothy Vick	Vick	scarlet	crimson	plain
Douglas Breadmore	Breadmore	purple flake	purple flake	plain

APPENDIX. 147

NAME.	RAISER, INTRODUCER.	COLOUR OF STANDARD.	COLOUR OF WINGS.	PLAIN OR WAVED.
Douglas Unwin	Unwin	maroon	maroon	waved
Duchess	Clark	salmon	salmon	waved
Duchess of Edinburgh	Eckford	orange, flushed crimson	rose	plain
Duchess of Sutherland	Eckford	pearl, suffused pink	pearl, suffused pink	plain
Duchess of Westminster	Eckford	apricot, flushed pink	rose	plain
Duchess of York	Eckford	white, pink stripes	white, pink stripes	plain
Dudley Lees	Breadmore	maroon	maroon	plain
Duke of Clarence	Eckford	rosy claret	rose	plain
Duke of Sutherland	Eckford	claret	indigo	plain
Duke of Westminster	Eckford	purplish rose	violet	plain
Duke of York	Eckford	rose	white	plain
Dusky Monarch	Breadmore	purplish maroon	purplish maroon	waved
E. C. Matthews	H. J. Jones	maroon	maroon	waved
E. J. Castle	Unwin	carmine, orange shading	deep rose	waved
Earl Cromer	Eckford	crimson lake	rosy lilac	plain
Earl of Plymouth	Bakers	buff	buff	waved
Earliest of All	Burpee	rose	white	plain
Earliest White	Burpee	white	white	plain
Earl Spencer	Cole	salmon	salmon	waved
Edna Unwin	Unwin	orange	rosy orange	waved
Edrom Beauty	Simpson, Malcolm, Dobbie	orange	orange, pink	waved
Elegance	Stark	white, feathered orange	white, feathered orange	plain
Elfrida	Johnson	primrose, rosy flakes	primrose, rosy flakes	plain
Eliza Eckford	Eckford	rose	rose	plain
Elsie Herbert	Breadmore	white, pink edge	white, pink edge	waved
Emily Eckford	Eckford	blue, suffused mauve	blue, suffused mauve	plain
Emily Henderson	Henderson	white	white	plain
Emily Lynch	Lynch	rose	buff, tinted pink	plain
Empress of India	Eckford	rose	white	plain
Enchantress	Stark	pink	pink	waved
Enid	Hemus	blue	blue	waved

148　　　*A BOOK ABOUT SWEET PEAS.*

NAME.	RAISER, INTRODUCER.	COLOUR OF STANDARD.	COLOUR OF WINGS.	PLAIN OR WAVED.
Eric Hinton	Hinton Bros.	pink	pink	waved
Ernest King	E. W. King & Co.	orange pink	pink	waved
Etna	Laxton	claret	purple	plain
Etta Dyke	Breadmore	white	white	waved
Evelyn Breadmore	Breadmore	white, tinged pink	white	plain
Evelyn Byatt	Watkins & Simpson	orange	rose	plain
Evelyn Hemus	Hemus	cream, pink edge	cream, pink edge	waved
Evening Star	Morse, Vaughan	primrose, pink shading	pink	plain
Exquisite	Bath	white, veined blue	white, veined blue	plain
Fadeless Scarlet Gem	Morse	scarlet	scarlet	plain
Fairy Queen	Haage & Schmidt	white, tinted pink	white	plain
Fascination	Eckford	magenta mauve	magenta	plain
Fashion	Morse, Burpee	rosy magenta	rosy magenta	plain
Finetta Bathurst	Bathurst, Mackereth	white	white	plain
Firefly	Eckford	crimson	crimson	plain
Fire King	see Firefly.			
Flora Norton	Morse, Vaughan	bright blue	blue	plain
Flora Norton Spencer	Morse	bright blue	blue	waved
Florence Frazer	Vaughan	rosy crimson	white	plain
Florence Molyneux	Dobbie & Co.	white, suffused carmine	white	plain
Florence Morse Spencer	Morse	blush	blush	waved
Florence Wright	Stark	white	white	slightly waved
Florrie Crutcher	A. J. Jones	rose, pink viens	rose	plain
Frank Dolby	Unwin, Watkins	lavender	lavender	slightly waved
F. R. Castle	Castle	crimson	crimson	waved
Frank Unwin	Unwin	lavender, shaded mauve	lavender, shaded mauve	waved
F. T. Beck	Bakers	pearl	pearl	plain
F. Woodward	Bakers	rosy mauve	rosy mauve	waved
Gaiety	Eckford	white, rose stripes	white, rose stripes	plain
George Baxter	Bolton	maroon	violet	waved
George Gordon	Eckford	claret red	rosy purple	plain
George Herbert	Breadmore	rosy carmine	carmine	waved
George Stark	Stark	scarlet	scarlet	waved

APPENDIX. 149

NAME.	RAISER, INTRODUCER.	COLOUR OF STANDARD.	COLOUR OF WINGS.	PLAIN OR WAVED.
Giant Cream Waved	Wm. Deal	cream	cream	waved
Gipsy Queen	Watkins and Simpson	buff, carmine flakes	buff, carmine flakes	waved
Gladys Deal	see Mrs. Higginson, Jun.			
Gladys French	Unwin	white, marbled blue	white, marbled blue	plain
Gladys Burt	Unwin	salmon pink, primrose ground	pink, primrose ground	waved
Glitters	Lumley	orange	orange	slightly waved
Golden Beauty	see America.			
Golden Gate	Morse, Burpee	lilac, deeper edge	lilac	plain
Golden Gleam	Sunset Co.	primrose	primrose	plain
Golden Rose	Morse, Burpee	primrose, pink flakes	primrose, pink flakes	plain
Gordon Ankentell	Breadmore	flame	flame	waved
Gorgeous	Morse, Burpee	orange	rose	plain
Gracie Greenwood	Eckford	cream, shaded pink	cream	plain
Grand Blue	see Captain of the Blues.			
Grey Friar	Morse, Burpee	white, purple flakes	white, purple flakes	plain
Grenadier	Clark	scarlet	scarlet	waved
Gwendoline	House	blue	blue	waved
H. J. R. Digges	Eckford	claret	claret	plain
Hannah Dale	Dobbie	maroon	maroon	plain
Harold	House	primrose	primrose	plain
Helen Grosvenor	Aldersey	orange and old rose	salmon rose	waved
Helen Lewis	Watson, Breadmore	orange	salmon	waved
Helen Pierce	Morse	blue veined	blue veined	plain
Hello Paradise	Hemus	heliotrope	heliotrope	waved
Henry Eckford	Eckford	salmon	salmon	plain
Herbert Marple	Marple	carmine rose	rose	waved
Herbert Smith	Holmes, Sydenham	orange	rose	plain
Hereward	Stark	pale cerise	pale cerise	waved
Her Majesty	Eckford	rose	pink	plain
Hester	Hemus	white, flaked blue	white, flaked blue	plain
Hetty Green	Ward, Bolton	orange scarlet	rose	plain

A BOOK ABOUT SWEET PEAS.

NAME.	RAISER, INTRODUCER.	COLOUR OF STANDARD.	COLOUR OF WINGS.	PLAIN OR WAVED.
Hetty Turner	Stark	pink	pink	waved
Hilda Jeffery	Breadmore	rose, shaded cream	rose, shaded cream	plain
Holdfast Belle	Hemus	pink, tinged apricot	pink	waved
Holdfast Pink	Hemus	buff pink	pink	waved
Hon. F. Bouverie	Eckford	coral pink	pink	plain
Hon. C. R. Spencer	see Helen Lewis.			
Hon. Mrs. Delia Spencer	Cole	pink	pink	waved
Hon. Mrs. E. Kenyon	Eckford	primrose	primrose	plain
Horace Skipper	Stark	rosy pink	pink	waved
Horace Wright	Eckford	violet	violet	plain
Ida Townsend	Jarman	rosy mauve	rosy mauve	waved
Ignea	Eckford	fiery red	rose	plain
Imperial Blue	Eckford	purplish blue	blue	plain
Improved Lucy Hemus	Hemus	crushed strawberry	crushed strawberry	waved
Indigo King	Eckford	purplish maroon	blue	plain
Invincible Black		very dark purple	dark purple	plain
Invincible Carmine	Laxton	carmine	carmine	plain
Invincible Scarlet	S. Brown, Carter	fiery red	fiery red	plain
Invincible Striped	Carter	red striped	red striped	plain
Isa Eckford	Eckford	cream, suffused pink	pink	plain
Ivy Herbert	Breadmore	plum	purple	waved
Jack Unwin	Unwin	rose flake	rose flake	waved
James Grieve	Eckford	sulphur	sulphur	plain
Janet Scott	Morse, Burpee	pink	pink	plain
Jeannie Gordon	Eckford	carmine rose	creamy buff	plain
Jessie Cuthbertson	Dobbie & Co.	cream, rose flakes	cream, rose flakes	plain
Jet	Aldersey, Sydenham	maroon	maroon	waved
John Ingman	Cole	carmine rose	rose	waved
John Watts, Sen.	see John Ingman.			
Josephine White	Ferry	white	white	plain
J. T. Crier	Breadmore	lavender	lavender	slightly waved
J. T. Taylor	Breadmore	plum	plum	waved

APPENDIX.

NAME.	RAISER, INTRODUCER.	COLOUR OF STANDARD.	COLOUR OF WINGS.	PLAIN OR WAVED.
Juanita	Morse, Burpee	white, striped lavender	white, striped lavender	plain
Katherine Tracey	Ferry	pink	pink	plain
Kathleen Macgowan	Breadmore	bright blue	blue	waved
Keston Red	H. J. Jones	scarlet	scarlet	plain
King Alfonso	Breadmore	crimson	crimson	waved
King Edward VII.	Eckford	crimson	crimson	plain
King Edward Spencer	Burpee	crimson	crimson	waved
Kitty Clive	Bolton	salmon scarlet	salmon scarlet	waved
Kitty Crier	Breadmore	rose	blush	waved
Kitty Eckford	Eckford	rose	rose	waved
Lady Aberdare	Breadmore	pink	pink	plain
Lady Althorp	Cole	pale blush	white	waved
Lady Beaconsfield	Eckford	salmon rose	buff	plain
Lady Cooper	Breadmore	lavender	lavender	plain
Lady Farren	Stark	rosy pink	pink	waved
Lady Grizel Hamilton	Eckford	lavender	lavender	hooded
Lady Hatherton	Cole	pale pink	pale pink	waved
Lady Lennard	H. J. Jones	white	white	waved
Lady Mary Currie	Eckford	orange pink	pink	plain
Lady M. Ormsby Gore	Eckford	buff, pink tint	buff, pink tint	plain
Lady Nina Balfour	Eckford	lavender	lavender	plain
Lady Penzance	Eckford	rose	rose	plain
Lady Pollock	Gilbert	pink	pink	waved
Lady Sarah Spencer	Cole	salmon pink	salmon pink	waved
Lady Skelmersdale	Eckford	rosy lilac	blush	plain
Lavender George Herbert	Breadmore	lavender	lavender	waved
Lady Treloar	Dobble & Co.	rosy mauve	rosy mauve	plain
Lemon Queen	Eckford	blush, tinted salmon	blush	plain
Liberty	Lumley	crimson	crimson	waved
Little Dorrit	Eckford	carmine	white	plain
Lizette Lumley	Lumley	rose flake	rose flake	waved
Lord Althorp	Cole	orange	salmon	waved

A BOOK ABOUT SWEET PEAS.

NAME.	RAISER, INTRODUCER.	COLOUR OF STANDARD.	COLOUR OF WINGS.	PLAIN OR WAVED.
Lord Kenyon	Eckford	rosy magenta	rose	plain
Lord Nelson	House	dark blue	dark blue	plain
Lord Rosebery	Eckford	bright rose	rose	plain
Lorna Doone	Stark	blush	blush	waved
Lottie Eckford	Eckford	white, blue edge	white, blue edge	plain
Lottie Hutchins	Morse, Burpee	primrose, pink stripes	primrose	plain
Lovely	Eckford	pink	pink	plain
Lovely Spencer	Morse	pink	pink	waved
Lucy Hemus	Hemus	carmine rose	creamy buff	waved
Madame Carnot	Laxton	blue	blue	plain
Madeline Cole	Stark	pale lavender	pale lavender	plain
Maggie Stark	Stark	orange	salmon	waved
Magnificent	Miller	scarlet and white flake	flake	waved
Maid of Honour	Morse, Burpee	white, edged lilac	white, edged lilac	plain
Majestic	Morse, Burpee	rosy red	rose	plain
Marbled Blue	Sutton	white, flaked blue	white, flaked blue	plain
Marchioness of Cholmondeley	Eckford	creamy buff	cream, pink tinge	plain
Marie Corelli	Burpee	rose	rose	waved
Marjory Linzee	Breadmore	rosy pink	rosy pink	waved
Marjorie Willis	Lumley	rich rose	rose	waved
Maroon Paradise	Hemus	maroon	maroon	waved
Mars	Eckford	fiery red	red	plain
Masterpiece	Malcolm, Dobbie	lavender, tinted rose	lavender	waved
Maud Guest	Eckford	blush white	white	waved
Mauve Paradise	Hemus	pale mauve	pale mauve	waved
Mauve Queen	Eckford	mauve	mauve	plain
May Malcolm	Malcolm	salmon pink	salmon pink	waved
May Perrett	Eckford	ivory	ivory	plain
Memento	see Flora Norton			
Menie Christie	Dobbie & Co.	rosy magenta	rosy magenta	waved
Mercia	Stark	salmon	salmon	waved
Meteor	Eckford	salmon	rose	plain

APPENDIX.

NAME.	RAISER, INTRODUCER.	COLOUR OF STANDARD.	COLOUR OF WINGS.	PLAIN OR WAVED.
Mid-Blue	Sutton, Eckford	sky blue	sky blue	plain
Mikado	Eckford	striped crimson and white	striped	plain
Mildred Ward	Ward, Sydenham	orange	orange	plain
Millie Maslin	Holmes, Sydenham	maroon	maroon	plain
Mima Johnston	Eckford	rosy carmine	rose	plain
Miriam Beaver	Burpee	salmon pink, primrose ground	pink	waved
Miss B. Whiley		orange	rose	plain
Miss Bostock		creamy pink	cream	waved
Miss Doris	see Doris Cannell.			
Miss E. F. Drayson	Unwin	scarlet	scarlet	waved
Miss Frills	Gilbert	blush	blush	waved
Miss Hunt	Eckford	salmon, rose	rose	plain
Miss H. C. Philbrick	Stark	deep blue	blue	plain
Miss L. E. King	E. W. King & Co.,	cream, flaked rose	flaked	waved
Miss Violet Fellowes	Hobbies	orange	rosy salmon	waved
Miss Willmott	Eckford	salmon pink	salmon pink	plain
Modesty	Morse, Burpee	white, shaded pink	pale pink	plain
Monarch	Eckford	bronzy red	blue	plain
Mont Blanc	Benary	white	white	plain
Mother O'Pearl	Aldersey, Sydenham	silvery lavender	silvery	waved
Mrs. Andrew Ireland	Dobbie & Co.	rose	blush	waved
Mrs. A. Malcolm	Malcolm, Mackereth	cream	cream	waved
Mrs. A. Norris	H. J. Jones	rich rose	rose	waved
Mrs. Alec Ware	R. Bolton	cream, shaded apricot	cream	waved
Mrs. Alfred Watkins	Unwin, Watkins	pale pink	pale pink	waved
Mrs. Bieberstedt	Bell & Bieberstedt	rosy lilac	lilac	plain
Mrs. Charles Foster	Bakers	lavender, shaded rose	lavender	waved
Mrs. C. Mander	Bakers	magenta	magenta	waved
Mrs. Chic Holmes	H. J. Jones	rosy mauve	rose	waved
Mrs. Collier	Dobbie & Co.	primrose	primrose	plain
Mrs. C. W. Breadmore	Breadmore	primrose, pink edge	primrose, pink edge	waved
Mrs. Duncan	Stark	crimson	crimson	waved
Mrs. Dugdale	Eckford	rose	pink	plain

154 A BOOK ABOUT SWEET PEAS.

NAME.	RAISER, INTRODUCER.	COLOUR OF STANDARD.	COLOUR OF WINGS.	PLAIN OR WAVED.
Mrs. Eckford	Eckford	primrose	primrose	plain
Mrs. E. Herbert	H. J. Jones	pinkish lilac	lilac	plain
Mrs. Fitzgerald	Eckford	cream, edged rose	cream	plain
Mrs. Gladstone	Eckford	pink	blush	plain
Mrs. G. Charles	R. Bolton	blue	blue	waved
Mrs. G. Higginson, Jun.	Morse, Vaughan	lavender	lavender	plain
Mrs. Godfrey Baring	see Mrs. Collier.			
Mrs. Hardcastle Sykes	R. Bolton	blush	blush	waved
Mrs. Henry Bell	R. Bolton	cream, pink border	cream, pink border	waved
Mrs. H. K. Barnes	Dobbie & Co.	apricot	creamy buff	plain
Mrs. Hugh Dickson	Dobbie & Co.	cream, rose border	cream, rose border	waved
Mrs. J. Miller	H. J. Jones	salmon pink	salmon pink	plain
Mrs. Miller	Miller	primrose	primrose	waved
Mrs. J. G. Day	H. J. Jones	primrose	primrose	waved
Mrs. J. Chamberlain	Eckford	white, striped rose	white, striped rose	plain
Mrs. J. Chamberlain Spencer	Morse, Burpee	white, striped rose	white, striped rose	waved
Mrs. Kenrick	Bakers	salmon pink	pink	plain
Mrs. Knights Smith	Eckford	pink	pink	plain
Mrs. Lumley	Lumley	cream, centre flaked	cream	waved
Mrs. P. J. Foley	H. J. Jones	lavender	lavender	plain
Mrs. E. Noakes	Agate	lavender	lavender	waved
Mrs. R. Cannell	Cannell	pink	pink	waved
Mrs. R. C. Pulling	H. J. Jones	white, tinted red	white	waved
Mrs. R. F. Felton	R. Bolton	primrose	primrose	plain
Mrs. Rothera	see Sutton's Queen			
Mrs. R. M. Shelton	Bakers	rosy carmine	rose	waved
Mrs. Routzahn	Burpee	cream, pink border	cream, pink border	waved
Mrs. R. W. Pitt	Stark	crushed strawberry	crushed strawberry	waved
Mrs. T. G. Baker	Bakers	white, bronzy edge	white	waved
Mrs. Sankey	Eckford	white	white	plain
Mrs. Sankey Spencer	Morse	white	white	waved

APPENDIX.

NAME.	RAISER, INTRODUCER.	COLOUR OF STANDARD.	COLOUR OF WINGS.	PLAIN OR WAVED.
Mrs. Tigwell	Tigwell	cream, rose stripe	striped	waved
Mrs. Tom Fagg	H. J. Jones	mauve, tinted pink	mauve	slightly waved
Mrs. Walter Carter	Bunting	lavender	lavender	waved
Mr. Walter Wright	Eckford	mauve	blue	plain
Mrs. W. Wright Spencer	Routzahn	mauve	blue	waved
Mrs. W. J. Unwin	Unwin	white, orange flakes	white, orange flakes	plain
Mrs. W. King	E. W. King & Co.	rosy carmine	rose	waved
Mrs. Townsend	Jarman	white, violet border	white, violet border	waved
Mrs. Wilcox	Gilbert & Son	white, striped red	white, striped red	waved
Money Maker	Agate	white	white	waved
Nancy Perkin	Perkin	salmon	salmon	waved
Navy Blue	Burpee	dark blue	dark blue	plain
Navy Blue Spencer	Breadmore	dark blue	dark blue	waved
Negro	H. J. Jones	maroon	maroon	waved
Nell Gwynn	Stark	pink, cream ground	pink, cream ground	waved
New Countess	Burpee	lavender	lavender	plain
Nigger	House & Co.	dark purple	dark purple	plain
Nora Unwin	Unwin, Watkins	white	white	waved
Norma	Clark	blush, pink edge	blush, pink edge	waved
Novelty	Eckford	orange	mauve	plain
Nubian	House	chocolate	chocolate	waved
Nymphaea	Morse, Vaughan	white turning pink	white	plain
Oddity	Morse, Burpee	pink, crimson veins	pink	plain
Olive Bolton	R. Bolton	pink	pink	waved
Olive Ruffell	Stark	rose	rose	waved
Opal	Aldersey, Sydenham	pale lavender	lavender	waved
Orange Countess	see Helen Lewis.			
Orange Prince	Eckford	orange	pink	plain
Orange King	Bide	orange	orange	waved
Oregonia	Walker	white, striped red	white, striped red	hooded
Oriental	Morse, Burpee	orange pink	orange pink	plain
Othello	Eckford	chocolate	chocolate	plain

156 A BOOK ABOUT SWEET PEAS.

NAME.	RAISER, INTRODUCER.	COLOUR OF STANDARD.	COLOUR OF WINGS.	PLAIN OR WAVED.
Othello Spencer	Burpee	maroon	maroon	waved
Ovid	Eckford	rosy red	rose	plain
Oxford Stripe	Sutton	white, flaked blue	white, flaked blue	plain
Painted Lady		rose	white	plain
Paradise	Hemus, Sydenham	pink	pink	waved
Paradise Apple Blossom	Hemus	apple blossom	apple blossom	waved
Paradise Beauty	Hemus	ivory	ivory	waved
Paradise Bicolor	Hemus	pink	blush	waved
Paradise Blue Flake	Hemus	white, flaked blue	white, flaked blue	waved
Paradise Carmine	Hemus	rosy carmine	rose	waved
Paradise Ivory	Hemus	ivory	ivory	waved
Paradise Opal	Hemus	heliotrope	heliotrope	waved
Paradise Red Flake	Hemus	white, flaked red	white, flaked red	waved
Paradise Regained	Hemus	blush	white	waved
Paradise Sunrise	Hemus	lemon, suffused blush	lemon, suffused blush	waved
Peach Blossom	Eckford	salmon pink	pink	plain
Peacock	H. J. Jones	red	blue	plain
Perdita	Bath	white, marbled pink	white, marbled pink	plain
Phenomenal	Morse	white, blue edge	white, blue edge	plain
Phœnix	E. W. King & Co.	white, shaded lilac	white, shaded lilac	waved
Phyllis Unwin	Unwin, Watkins	rosy carmine	rose	waved
Picotee	Watkins and Simpson	white, edged carmine	white, edged carmine	waved
Pink Friar	Morse, Burpee	white, marbled rose	white, marbled rose	plain
Pink Gem	Breadmore	blush	blush	waved
Pink Pearl	Unwin	pink	pink	waved
Pride of Coombe	House	silvery, flaked rose	silvery, flaked rose	waved
Pride of St. Albans	Ryder	pink	pink	waved
Prima Donna	Eckford	pink	pink	plain
Primrose	Eckford	primrose	primrose	plain
Primrose Paradise	Hemus	primrose	primrose	waved
Primrose Spencer	Breadmore	primrose	primrose	waved
Primrose Spencer	Burpee	primrose	primrose	waved

APPENDIX. 157

NAME.	RAISER, INTRODUCER.	COLOUR OF STANDARD.	COLOUR OF WINGS.	PLAIN OR WAVED.
Primrose Waved	Eckford	primrose	primrose	waved
Prince Edward of York	Eckford	crimson	rose	plain
Prince of Asturias	Breadmore	maroon	purple	waved
Prince of Wales	Eckford	rose	rose	plain
Prince of Wales Spencer	Burpee	carmine rose	carmine rose	waved
Prince Olaf	Dobbie & Co.	white, blue flakes	white, blue flakes	plain
Princess Beatrice	Muskett, Hurst	pink	pink	plain
Princess Ena	Eckford	purplish mauve	mauve	waved
Princess Juliana	Breadmore	primrose	primrose	waved
Princess May	Laxton	light mauve	lavender	plain
Princess of Wales	Eckford	white, mauve stripes	white, mauve stripes	plain
Princess Maud of Wales	Eckford	pale cerise	pale cerise	plain
Princess Victoria	Dobbie & Co.	blush	blush	waved
Princess Victoria	Eckford	cerise	pink	plain
Purity	R. Bolton, Sharpe	white	white	waved
Purple King	Eckford	purple	indigo	plain
Purple Paradise	Hemus	purple	purple	waved
Purple Prince	Eckford	maroon	purple	plain
Queen	See Sutton's Queen.			
Queen	Clark	cream, pink border	cream, pink border	waved
Queen Alexandra	Eckford	scarlet	scarlet	plain
Queenie	Wm. Deal	buff	buff	waved
Queen of England	Eckford	white	white	plain
Queen of Norway	R. Bolton	purplish mauve	mauve	waved
Queen of Pinks	Sutton	pink	pink	plain
Queen of Spain	Eckford	pearly pink	pearly pink	plain
Queen of Spain Spencer	Eckford	pearly pink	pearly pink	waved
Queen of the Isles	Eckford	white, striped crimson	white, striped crimson	plain
Queen Victoria	Eckford	primrose	primrose	plain

158 A BOOK ABOUT SWEET PEAS.

NAME.	RAISER, INTRODUCER.	COLOUR OF STANDARD.	COLOUR OF WINGS.	PLAIN OR WAVED.
Queen Victoria Spencer	Burpee	primrose	primrose	waved
Ramona	Morse, Burpee	white, flaked pink	white, flaked pink	plain
Ramona Spencer	Morse	white, flaked pink	white, flaked pink.	waved
Red Riding Hood	Sunset Co.	pink and white	pink and white	plain
Reggie Breadmore	Breadmore	purple flake	purple flake	plain
Regina	R. Bolton, Sharpe	maroon	maroon	waved
Rising Sun	Laxton	salmon rose	pale pink	plain
Romani Ronni	Aldersey, Sydenham	cream and pink	cream and pink	waved
Romola Plazzani	Eckford	violet blue	violet blue	plain
Rosabelle Hoare	Unwin	white, rose flake	white, rose flake	waved
Rosalind	Clark	rose	rose	waved
Rose Queen	Stark	rose	rose	plain
Rosie Adams	Stevenson, H. J. Wright			
Rosie Gilbert	Gilbert & Son	violet	rose	waved
Rosie Sydenham	Burpee, Sydenham	rosy carmine	rose	waved
Rosy Morn	Cannell	rose	rose	waved
Royal Robe	Eckford	rose	rose	waved
Royal Rose	Eckford	pink	blush	plain
Ruby	Aldersey	rose	rose	plain
Sadie Burpee	Eckford	orange	rose	waved
St. George	Hurst & Son	white	white	plain
Salopian	Eckford	orange	rose	slightly waved
Salvation Lassie	Burpee	crimson	crimson	hooded
Scarlet Gem	Eckford	carmine	carmine	plain
Scotch Pearl	Aldersey	scarlet	scarlet	plain
Senator	Eckford	heliotrope	heliotrope	waved
Senator Spencer	Burpee	heliotrope, purple flakes	flaked	plain
Sensation	Morse, Burpee	heliotrope, claret flakes	heliotrope, claret flakes	waved
Severn Queen	Hemus	blush	white	plain
Shahzada	Eckford	primrose	primrose	plain
Shasta	Morse	purplish maroon	maroon	plain
		white	white	plain

APPENDIX.

NAME.	RAISER, INTRODUCER.	COLOUR OF STANDARD.	COLOUR OF WINGS.	PLAIN OR WAVED.
Shawondasee	Hemus	blue	blue	waved
Silas Cole	Cole	maroon	maroon	waved
Silver Wings	Stark & Son	white, pink flakes	white, flaked	waved
Snapdragon	Morse, Burpee	pink and white	pink and white	plain
Snowflake	Breadmore	white	white	waved
Speckled Beauty	Morse, Vaughan	primrose, marbled red	primrose, marbled red	plain
Splendour	Eckford	rose	rose	plain
Stanley	Eckford	maroon	maroon	plain
Stella Morse	Morse, Burpee	buff, tinted pink	buff	plain
Stirling Stent	Agate	salmon	salmon	waved
Sue Earl	Morse, Burpee	primrose, shading to mauve	primrose	waved
Suffragette	House	white, pencilled blue	white, pencilled blue	plain
Sunbeams	Morse, Burpee	primrose	primrose	waved
Sunproof Crimson	Dobbie & Co.	crimson	crimson	waved
Sunproof Crimson	Holmes, Sydenham	crimson	crimson	waved
Sunproof King Alfonso	Breadmore	crimson	crimson	waved
Sunproof Saloplan	Burpee	crimson	crimson	plain
Sunrise	Morse, Vaughan	pink, primrose ground	pink	waved
Sunrise	Gilbert & Son	orange pink	pink	plain
Sunset	Morse, Vaughan	primrose, rose stripes	striped	waved
Sutton's Queen	Rothera, Sutton	cream, pink border	cream, pink border	plain
Sweet Lavender	Bath	lavender	lavender	plain
Sybil Eckford	Eckford	lemon, blush suffusion	lemon	plain
Syeira Lee	Aldersey, Sydenham	cream, rose border	cream, rose border	waved
Tennant Spencer	Morse	mauve	mauve	plain
The Belle	Eckford	rose, flaked crimson	rose	plain
The Bride	Lynch	white	white	plain
The Fairy	Johnson	lavender, white	lavender, white	waved
The King	Dobbie & Co.	crimson	crimson	waved
The Marquis	Dobbie & Co.	rosy mauve	rosy mauve	plain
The Queen	Eckford	rosy pink, shaded mauve	rosy lavender	waved
Thora	Stark	pink	pink	waved
Tom Bolton	Bolton	maroon	maroon	waved

NAME.	RAISER, INTRODUCER.	COLOUR OF STANDARD.	COLOUR OF WINGS.	PLAIN OR WAVED.
Topaz	Aldersey	cream	cream	waved
Toreador	see America.			
Tortoise Shell	Aldersey	salmon	salmon	waved
Triumph	Eckford	pink	white	plain
Triumph Spencer	R. Bolton	salmon pink	blush	waved
Tweedy Smith	Breadmore	rose	blush	plain
Unique	Stark & Son	white, flaked blue	white, flaked blue	plain
Venus	Eckford	buff, suffused salmon	buff	plain
Vera Jeffrey	Breadmore	blush	blush	waved
Vesuvius	J. C. Schmidt	claret	claret	plain
Viola Ratcliffe	Breadmore	blush	blush	waved
Violet Queen	Carter	violet	violet	plain
Waved Cream	Malcolm, Mackereth	cream	cream	waved
Waverley	Eckford	rosy claret	blue	plain
Wawona	Morse, Burpee	white, lilac stripes	striped	plain
White Paradise	Hemus	white	white	waved
White Spencer	Burpee	white	white	waved
White Spencer	Dobbie & Co.	white	white	waved
White Triumph	Hemus	white	white	waved
White Waved	Eckford	white	white	plain
White Wonder	Morse, Burpee	white	white	waved
Winnie Cleve	H. J. Jones	mauve	blue	plain
Winnie Jones	Stark	cream, rose flakes	flaked	plain
Winsome	Wm. Deal	pink, suffused heliotrope	pink, suffused heliotrope	waved
Winifred Deal	Wm. Deal	white, rose edge	white, rose edge	waved
W. T. Hutchins	Burpee	blush pink, lemon centre	blush	waved
Yellow Hammer	Breadmore	primrose	primrose	waved
Zara	Hemus	salmon pink	pink	plain
Zarina	Hemus	pale pink	pale pink	waved
Zephyr	Biffen, Hemus	blue	blue	waved
Zero	Hemus	white	white	plain
Zoe	Biffen, Unwin	blue	blue	plain

SELECTIONS OF SWEET PEAS.

The hundreds of varieties of Sweet Peas in the preceding catalogue present a bewildering array to the beginner. He might wander up and down the columns interminably, never getting nearer his goal of a dozen or two of reliable sorts for his garden. Nor is the would-be exhibitor in much better case.

Let us see if we can make a few useful selections from the list, overcoming the momentary hesitation which arises from the fact that the constant inrush of new varieties tends to put selections out of date almost as soon as they are made. That is a thing which the author of a book cannot help. He must do the best he can with the material which is available at the time he passes his pages for press.

SWEET PEAS FOR THE GARDEN.

There is not the same difference between garden and exhibition Sweet Peas as there is between garden and show Roses; or, to put it in another way, there are not so many cases in which a variety that is good for the garden is unsuitable for the exhibition table. This arises from the fact that there is not much variation in the habit or degree of floriferousness of Sweet Peas. In reality, garden and show sorts are practically interchangeable. None the less it may be well to give a selection of varieties which, with good culture, are admirable garden varieties. Here are thirty:

- A. J. Cook
- Aurora Spencer.
- Black Knight.
- Colleen.
- Constance Oliver.
- Countess Spencer.
- Dora Breadmore.
- Dorothy Eckford.
- Duke of Westminster.
- E. J. Castle.
- Frank Dolby.
- Gladys Burt.
- Helen Lewis.
- Helen Pierce.
- James Grieve.
- King Edward VII.
- Lady Althorp.
- Lady Grizel Hamilton.
- Lord Nelson.
- Marjorie Willis.
- Masterpiece.
- Menie Christie.
- Miss Willmott.
- Mrs. C. W. Breadmore
- Nora Unwin.
- Prince Olaf.
- Queen Alexandra.
- Sunproof Crimson.
- Tennant Spencer.
- Winsome.

The foregoing varieties comprise all the principal colours. Each is fully described in the table. To get a list of twelve only, we might take:

- Black Knight.
- Countess Spencer.
- Duke of Westminster.
- Frank Dolby.
- Helen Lewis.
- Helen Pierce.
- James Grieve.
- Lord Nelson.
- Nora Unwin.
- Queen Alexandra.
- Sunproof Crimson.
- Winsome.

These give the desired diversity of colour.

SWEET PEAS FOR EXHIBITION.

We have already seen that for show we want varieties bearing fours, and we must draw mainly from the waved section to get this quality in combination with large size. The following would be a good selection of thirty:

A. J. Cook.
Asta Ohn.
Audrey Crier.
Aurora Spencer.
Clara Curtis.
Constance Oliver.
Countess Spencer.
Douglas Unwin.
Earl Spencer.
Elsie Herbert.
Etta Dyke.
Frank Dolby.
George Stark.
Helen Lewis.
Helen Pierce.
John Ingman.
King Edward Spencer.
Lord Nelson.
Masterpiece.
Menie Christie.
Mrs. Andrew Ireland.
Mrs. C. W. Breadmore.
Mrs. Hardcastle Sykes.
Mrs. Hugh Dickson.
Paradise Ivory.
Prince of Asturias.
Princess Juliana.
Snowflake.
Sunproof Crimson.
Tennant Spencer.

The following would make a good twelve:

Asta Ohn.
Audrey Crier.
Clara Curtis.
Countess Spencer
Douglas Unwin.
Earl Spencer.
Etta Dyke.
George Stark.
Helen Lewis.
Mrs. C. W. Breadmore.
Sunproof Crimson.
Tennant Spencer.

The following would also make a good twelve:

Aurora Spencer.
Constance Oliver.
Elsie Herbert.
Earl Spencer.
King Edward Spencer.
Lord Nelson.
Masterpiece.
Mrs. Hardcastle Sykes.
Mrs. Hugh Dickson.
Prince of Asturias.
Princess Juliana.
Snowflake.

Sharp contrasts of colour are provided in the selections.

SEEDSMEN'S SELECTIONS.

I have said elsewhere that a feature of the Sweet Pea trade is the offer of special selections by seedsmen. Such selections are to be found in the catalogues of the seedsmen, and in advertisements in the horticultural papers. The varieties are named. The advantage of accepting seedsmen's selections is that good varieties are secured without the trouble of hunting through lists and at a low cost. The seeds are of the same quality as those sold separately.

TOO-MUCH-ALIKE VARIETIES.

By the rules of the National Sweet Pea Society the varieties bracketted may not be shown together in the same stand at the Society's Shows.

{ Etta Dyke
Paradise White.
Purity.
Snowflake.
White Spencer.
White waved.

{ Baker's Scarlet.
Miss E. F. Drayson
Queen Alexandra.
Scarlet Gem.

{ Albert Gilbert.
Lady Farren.
Marjorie Willis.
Rosalind.
Splendour Spencer.

{ Mrs. Townsend.
Phenomenal.

{ Anna Lumley.
Black Knight Spencer.
Douglas Unwin.
Maroon Paradise.
May Gerhold.
Nubian.
Othello Spencer.

{ Harold.
James Grieve.
Mrs. A. Malcolm.
Mrs. Collier.
Yellow Hammer.

{ Countess of Radnor.
Lady Grizel Hamilton.

{ Flora Norton.
Miss Philbrick.

{ Anglian Blue.
Flora Norton Spencer.
Kathleen Macgowan.
Zephyr.

{ E. J. Castle.
George Herbert.
John Ingman.
Mrs. W. King.
Paradise Carmine.
Phyllis Unwin.
Rosie Sydenham.
Rosy Morn.
Spencer Carmine.

{ Mid-Blue.
Zoe.

{ Clara Curtis.
Malcolm's Waved Cream.
Paradise Cream.
Primrose Paradise.
Primrose Waved.
Princess Juliana.
Primrose Spencer.

{ Evelyn Hemus.
Mrs. C. W. Breadmore.

{ Countess Spencer.
Enchantress.
Paradise.
Pink Pearl.

{ Hester.
Marbled Blue.

{ A. B. Bantock.
Earl of Plymouth.
Kitty Lea.
Mrs. Henry Bell.
Mrs. Hugh Dickson.
Sutton's Queen.
Romani Ronni.

{ Beauty (Bolton's).
Bobby K.
Countess of Northbrook.
Florence Morse Spencer.
Lorna Doone.
Mrs. Hardcastle Sykes.
Princess Victoria.

{ Dodwell F. Browne.
King Alfonso.
King Edward Spencer.
Paradise Crimson.
Rosie Gilbert.
Sunproof King Alfonso.
Sunproof Crimson (Dobbie's).
The King.

L'ENVOI.

With the completion of the catalogue and selections I complete my book on Sweet Peas. It is my earnest hope that it may help to spread the love of these beautiful flowers. It will go into the hands of people in all parts of the world. If it increases their interest or aids their culture, thus winning their sympathy, I hope that they will use it as an instrument for interesting and helping others. I hope, too, that those who are sufficiently interested will write to me—about the book, about Sweet Peas, about the influence of flowers on their lives,—about anything which is likely to link us together. I throw a tendril to any hard-pressed swimmer struggling with rough water, and draw him to the safety and peace of the garden.

Walter P. Wright.

Lyminge, Folkestone, England.

INDEX.

A.

A.B.C., Sweet Pea Grower's, 119-141.
Aldersey, Hugh, 141.
America, United States of, Sweet Peas in, 111-114, 119.
Annual, 120.
Annuals, 121.
Appendix, Varieties and Selections, 142-164.
Arkwright, Rev. E., 121.
Artificial Manures, 121.
Audit, 122.
Autumn sowing (see also "Sowing"), 72.

B.

Bakers, 122.
Bastard trenching, 48.
Bath, R. H. Ltd, 121.
Bathurst, R., 121.
Bees and Sweet Peas (illustrated), 26, 27.
Beetle in Sweet Pea flowers, 19, 27.
Bell and Bieberstedt, 121.
Bicentenary, 121.
Biffen, R. H., 121.
Birds, 84, 121.
Blight, 82.
Blue-edged (Blue Hybrid), 19.
Bolton, R., 121.
Breadmore, C. W., 122.
Bridgeford, J. M., 122.
Buds, 122.
Bunting, G. A., & Co., 122.
Burpee, W. Atlee, & Co., 122.
Bush, 122.

C.

California, seed-growing in, 111, 112.
Carnforth, 104.
Carter, J., & Co., 123.
Catalogue of varieties, 142-164.
Catalogues, 123.
Caterpillars, 84.
Chemical manures, 51.
Cheshire, Sweet Peas in, 104.
Christy, E. H., 123.
Clarke, Major Trevor, 123.
Classification, 123.
Clumps, 61, 123.
Cole, Silas, 124.
Colour, blends, 58, 59, 60, 61, 125.
Colour, good and bad, 61.
Colonies, Sweet Peas in, 110, 124.
Commelin, C., 125.
Cornwall, Sweet Peas in, 102.
Cottage gardens, Sweet Peas in, 93-97.
Countess Spencer, Origin of, 22.
Cross-fertilisation, 18, 24, (illustrated) 29.
Cupani, 14.
Cupid, 125.
Curtis, C. H., 125.
Cuthbertson, W., 126.

D.

Daniels Bros., 126.
Darlington, T. W., 126.
Deal, Wm., 126.
Devonshire, Sweet Peas in, 102.
Dicks, S. B., 126.
Dickson, A., & Sons, 126.
Digges, H. J. R., 126.
Dipnall, T. H., 126.
Diseases, 126.
Dobbie & Co., 126.
Dorset, Sweet Peas in, 102.
Double Sweet Peas, 127.
Drayson, G. F., 127.
Duncan, T., 127.
Duns as a Sweet Pea centre, 99.

E.

Eckford, Henry, 20, 103, 127.
Enemies of Sweet Peas, 79, 127.
Engelmann, G., 127.
Essex, 127.

Everlasting Pea, 128.
Exhibiting, Two sides to, 45.
   ,,   Notes on, 64-69, 128.
   ,,   Varieties for, 162.

F.

Fences, Sweet Peas on, 62.
Fertilisation (see also Cross and Self-Fertilisation), 129.
Fixing new Sweet Peas, 31, 130.
Floral Committee, 130.
Foster, C., 130.
Flowers, number on stem, 61.
   ,,   how to pack, 68.
Freshness, 61.

G.

Garden, Sweet Peas for, 161.
Gathering, 77 (*illustrated*), 129.
Germination, 131.
Gilbert & Son, 131.
Gladys Unwin, 22.
Green Fly, 83.
Gypsophila paniculata, 67.

H.

Hemus, Miss, 131.
Herbert, G., 131.
Hitchins, Martin F., 131.
Holmes, R., 131.
Hooded, 131.
House, I., & Son, 131.
Hurst & Son, 132.
Hutchins, Rev. W. T., 132.

I.

Insects (see also "Enemies"), 132.
Ireland, Andrew, 132.
   ,,   Sweet Peas in, 105, 106.

J.

Jones, H. J., 132.
   ,,   J., 132.
   ,,   T., 132.
Judging Sweet Peas, 66.

K.

King, E. W., & Co., 132.
   ,, J. K., & Sons, 132.

L.

Lathyrus, crossing, 32.
   ,, *latifolius*, 32.
Lathyrus magellanicus, 19.
   ,, *odoratus*, 15.
   ,, *sativus azureus*, 32.
Laxton, T., 133.
Leak, G. W., 133.
Leather-jacket grubs, 50.
Liquid manure, 49.
Lord Anson's Pea, 19, 32.
Lumley, Wm., 133.

M.

Mackereth, H. W., 133.
Malcolm, A., 133.
Manuring, 48, 49, 50.
Market, Sweet Peas for, 70-73.
Meligethes, 28.
Mendelism, 32, 133.
Mice, 84.
Mildew, 83.
Miller, S., 134.
Morse, C. C., & Co., 134.
Mould, 82.
Mulching, 51.

N.

National Sweet Pea Society, 134.
Nitrate of potash, 51.
   ,,   soda, 51.
Nitro-bacterine, 134.

P.

Packing, 68, 73, 135.
Painted Lady, 15.
Perfume of Sweet Peas, 9, 11.
Phosphate of potash, 51.
Planting, 52, 53, 135.
Plukenet, L., 135.
Pots, Sweet Peas in, 75.
Profit, Sweet Peas for, 70-73.
Properties, 135.

R.

Reading, 135.
Rogueing Sweet Peas, 31, 135.
Rooms, Sweet Peas for, 136.
Root-rot, 83.
Root worms, 84.
Rothera, T., & Co., 136.
Rows, 136.

S.

Saving seed, 137.
Scent, 137.

INDEX.

Scotland, Sweet Peas in, 98-100.
Sea sand for Sweet Peas, 97.
Seed, and seedling (*illustrated*), 40.
," autumn sowing, 43.
," chipping, 39.
," dark and light, 39.
," gathering pods, 38.
," ripe and unripe, 38.
," saving, 37, 41, 42, 43, 44.
," small, 39.
," sowing in pots (*illustrated*), 42.
," structure of, 39.
Self-fertilisation, 18.
Shading, 68, 137.
Simpson, Rev. M., 138.
Slugs, 81.
Smith Fletcher & Co.'s collapsible support, 56, 138.
Smith, Fletcher & Co., 138.
," Herbert, 138.
Soil, bastard trenching, 48.
," good and bad, 47, 48.
Sowing, see "Seed."
Spencer, 138.
Sports, 138.
Spot, 83.
Staking (*illustrated*), 54, 55.
Stark, G., & Son, 139.
Stevenson, T., 139.
Stem, length of, 61.
Sticks, 139.
Stopping, 139.
Streak, 83.
String supports, 56.
Suburban gardens, 62.
Sulphate of iron, 51.
," potash, 51.
Superphosphate, 49.
Sutton & Sons, 139.
Sweet Peas, A.B.C., 119-141.
," and bees (*illustrated*), 26, 27.
," as an exhibition flower, 64-69.
," at stage for cross-fertilisation (*illustrated*), 29.
," autumn sowing, 72.
," beauty of, 9.
," botanical names of, 15.
," chemical manures for, 49, 50, 51.

Sweet Peas, clumps of, 61.
," colour blends of, (*illustrated*), 58, 59, 60, 61.
," colours of, 10, 11.
," early varieties, 15, 77.
," enemies of, 79.
," first appearance of waved, 21.
," fixing, 31.
," flower after petals have gone (*illustrated*), 28.
," flower emasculated (*illustrated*), 29.
," for exhibition, 162.
," for the garden, 161.
," for market, 70-73.
," from cuttings, 46.
," grown in mixture, 95.
," in herbaceous borders, 57-63.
," in pots, stopping (*illustrated*), 76.
," in suburban gardens, 62.
," in tubs, 77.
," in the British Colonies, 107-110.
," in English cottage gardens, 93-97.
," in Irish gardens, 105, 106.
," in Scottish gardens, 98-100.
," in Wales and the West country, 101-104.
," in the United States of America, 111-114.
," introduction of, 13.
," judging, 66.
," liquid manure for, 49.
," Mendelian principles of heredity in, 32.
," native country of, 14.
," natural cross-fertilisation, 18, 30.
," on walls and fences, 57-63.
," origin of waved, 22.
," packing, 68, 73.
," perfume of, 9.
," planting, 52.
," points of, 67.

Sweet Peas, provision for self-fertilisation, 18.
," rise into favour of, 13.
," rogueing, 31.
," sea sand for, 97.
," seeds and sowing, 36-46.
," shading, 68.
," soil and manure for, 47-51.
," sports of, 18.
," structure of, 10, 25.
," supporting with stakes, 55.
," supporting with stakes and string (*illustrated*), 55.
," supporting with wire, 55.
," supporting with string, 56.
," too-much-alike, 163.
," under glass, 74-78.
," varieties of, 85-92.
," Woman's influence on, 115-118.
Sydenham's wire ladder support (*illustrated*), 56.
Synonyms, 66.
Sydenham, R., 140.

T.

Télemly Sweet Peas, 77.
Teschemacher, E., 140.
Thomas, Harry H., 140.
Too-much-alike Varieties, 140, 163.

Trellis work, Sweet Peas on, 62.
Trials, 140.
Tubs, 140.

U.

Unwin, W. J., 140.
Uvedale, Dr., 14.

V.

Varieties, catalogue of, 142-164.
," notes on, 85-92.
," for market, 71.
Vase, Jones's Ideal (*illustrated*), 69.
Vases, Sweet Peas for, 140.

W.

Wales, Sweet Peas in, 101-104.
Walls, Sweet Peas on, 62.
Ward, H. E., 141.
," Sidney, 141.
Watkins & Simpson, 141.
Watson, J., Jun., 141.
Webb & Sons, 141.
Weevil, 82.
Wem, 103.
Winter-flowering, 141.
Wireworm, 50, 81.
Wire supports for, 55.
Woman's influence on Sweet Peas, 115-118.
Wrexham, 104.
Wright, Horace J., 141.
," Walter P., 141.

Z.

Zvolanek, A., 141.

AUDREY CRIER.
Salmon pink, a beautiful variety which has proved very unstable.
See Chapter XII.

ASTA OHN.
The waved lavender with rose tint. See Chapter XII.

MRS. CHARLES FOSTER.
Rosy lavender.   See Appendix.

A BOWL OF SWEET PEAS.
See Rooms. Chapter XX.

A VASE OF SWEET PEAS.
A charming ornament for a table.

AZURE FAIRY.
French grey and pale blue. See Appendix.

ZARINA.
A charming salmon pink. See Appendix.

ZERO.
A fine early white. See Appendix.

CONSTANCE OLIVER.
A lovely waved pink with primrose centre. See Chapter XII.

A TYPICAL POT OF SWEET PEAS,
This charming object has come from one seed.
See Chapter X.

SWEET PEAS GROWN IN FRONT OF A GARDEN SHED,
showing how an inartistic object may be screened.
See Chapter VII.

SWEET PEA AND ROSE BEAUTY.
A dark Sweet Pea, such as Mrs. Walter Wright, A. J. Cook or Duke of Westminster, near a pillar of Alister Stella Gray Rose.
(From the Author's Garden).

STAKING SWEET PEAS.
The magnificent row on the left is supported entirely by string, and is better than the right hand row, which is supported by sticks. These Peas won many important prizes.
See Chapter VI.

SWEET PEAS AT THE RIGHT STAGE FOR CROSS-FERTILISING OR GATHERING TO PACK.
See Chapters III. and IX.

A LOOSE SPIKE ON THE LEFT, A WELL-FILLED SPIKE ON THE RIGHT.
See Chapter VIII.

KING EDWARD SPENCER.
The American waved crimson. See Chapter XII.

JOHN INGMAN,
A fine waved carmine rose with orange in the standard.
See Chapter XII.

THE MARQUIS.
Waved mauve. See Chapter XII.

The magnificent exhibition variety,
SUNPROOF CRIMSON.
See Chapter XII.

SWEET PEA AND ROSE BEAUTY.
A pink Sweet Pea, such as Countess Spencer or Constance Oliver, near a pillar of The Lion Rose.
(From the Author's Garden).

PARADISE IVORY.
The photograph gives an excellent idea of the substance of this fine variety, but not of the waving. See Appendix.

HELEN PIERCE.
Veined blue, one of the most distinct and valuable of Sweet Peas,
See Chapter XII,

ETTA DYKE.
The grand white waved variety. See Chapter XII.

Photo.: Sutton & Sons, Reading].

AUTUMN SOWN SWEET PEAS,
with Southcote Old Manor House in the distance.   See Chapters IV. and IX.

A WEAK SWEET PEA PLANT,
such as results from thick culture, poor soil, or attack by enemies.
See Chapters IV. and XI.

SWEET PEA LEAVES EATEN BY A LOOPER CATERPILLAR.
See Chapter XI.

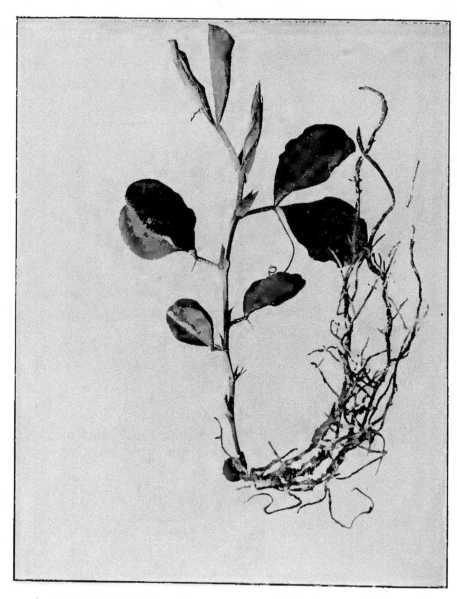

A STURDY WELL-ROOTED SWEET PEA SEEDLING,
Produced by good soil and thin culture. See Chapter IV.

RAISING SWEET PEAS IN POTS.

In the centre pots the seeds are well arranged; in the others they are too numerous and badly arranged. See Chapter IV.

BATH'S SWEET PEAS,

AWARDED LARGE GOLD . MEDAL .

NATIONAL SWEET PEA SOCIETY, 1909.

> We are not merely dealers in and advertisers of Sweet Peas but grow many acres for seed, and supply most of the wholesale houses in the trade. We conduct each season a trial of every leading variety in commerce, each occupying a row of 50 feet. These trials are visited by specialists and enthusiasts from all parts of the country, and we are glad to welcome visitors at any time during the flowering season.

We offer the following Novelties of our own raising for 1910.

DISTINCTION. White ground, distinctly edged rose red, an improved Elsie Herbert. Flower of beautiful form. Fixed. Per pkt. 1s.

AZURE FAIRY. French-grey, ground marbled pale blue, lovely and most dainty when seen in a bunch. Fixed. Per pkt. 1s.

PERDITH. White ground, marbled bright pink, a charming variety. Not quite fixed. Per pkt. 1s.

SWEET LAVENDER. White ground marbled lavender, a very pretty and distinct variety. Fixed. Per pkt. 1s.

> The three above marbled varieties are of the Helen Pierce type, and are splendid additions to the marbled section.
>
> Complete Catalogue of Sweet Peas containing all the leading varieties post free on application.

R. H. BATH, Ltd., The Floral Farms, WISBECH.

BOLTON'S Sweet Peas

THE FINEST – IN – THE WORLD.

909 AWARDS:
9 GOLD MEDALS and 2 SILVER CUPS.

ROBERT BOLTON has long Specialised in Sweet Peas and has raised such sterling novelties as Mrs. Hardcastle Sykes, voted by the leading Sweet Pea experts to be the best Sweet Pea in existence, Bolton's Pink, Mrs. Henry Bell, Clara Curtis, Tom Bolton, and many more of the leading varieties.

SEND DIRECT FOR TRUE STOCKS.
20 ACRES GROWN FOR SEED.

CATALOGUE containing sensational novelties and all the leading varieties post free.

Full cultural notes sent with every order.

ADDRESS IN FULL:

ROBERT BOLTON, The Sweet Pea Specialist,
WARTON, CARNFORTH.

"The Leading American Seed Catalogue."

Unlike any other,—it is now "Better than ever" for 1910!

AN ELEGANT BOOK OF 178 PAGES,—it is "THE SILENT SALESMAN" of the World's Largest Mail-Order Seed Trade. It tells the *plain truth* about the Best Seeds that can be grown,—as proved at our famous FORDHOOK FARMS,—the largest, most complete Trial Grounds in America. Handsomely bound with covers lithographed in nine colours it shows, with the six coloured plates Nine Novelties and Specialties in unequalled Vegetables, and five finest Beautiful New Flowers, including two superb "Gold Medal" Spencer Sweet Peas, of which one is named "Marie Corelli" by permission of this popular English Novelist. These plates have been accurately painted from nature in Europe, California and at Fordhook.

With hundreds of illustrations from photographs and carefully written descriptions it is a SAFE GUIDE to success in the garden and should be consulted by every one who plants seeds, whether for pleasure or profit. While too costly a book to send unsolicited (except to our regular customers), we are pleased to mail it FREE to every one who *has a garden* and personally writes for it. Shall we mail YOU a copy? If so, kindly write your address plainly and mail,—**To-day!**

Burpee's "King Edward" Spencer.
Exactly Natural Size.

W. ATLEE BURPEE & CO., | Seed Growers.
PHILADELPHIA.

Seed Gardens and Trial Grounds at our famous FORDHOOK FARMS, Bucks County, Pa., SUNNYBROOK FARM in New Jersey, and The New BURPEE RANCH in California.

Your Garden not Complete without

𝔇eal's 𝔖weet 𝔓eas.

TRY
COLLEEN, WINSOME,
WINIFRED DEAL, QUEENIE,
for 1909-10.

Some Grand Novelties to follow as time goes on.
LIST POST FREE.

WM. DEAL, F.R.H.S.,
BROOKLANDS, KELVEDON, ESSEX.

THE "IDEAL" VASE
(Tom Jones' Patent—Registered No. 5981).

For gracefully and effectively staging
Sweet Peas and other Annuals, Carnations, Daffodils,
Gaillardias, etc.

DESIGNED AND PATENTED BY TOM JONES, RUABON.

The Top is made of the Best British Glass, and The Base of Aluminium Coloured Metal.

15/- Per Dozen.   8/- Per Half-Dozen.

PARTICULARS FROM
DOBBIE & Co., Seedsmen, Rothesay, N.B.
R. BOLTON, Sweet Pea Specialist, Warton, Carnforth.
W. J. UNWIN,   ,,   ,,   Histon, Cambs.
JONES & SON, Florists, Shrewsbury.
AND OTHER SWEET PEA SPECIALISTS.

COLLAPSIBLE
SWEET PEA TRAINERS.

(PATENT APPLIED FOR).

Growers of Sweet Peas have of late been using Circular Trainers in large numbers. These have been found difficult to store when not in use, and we have therefore brought out and patented a Collapsible Trainer, which goes into very small space when not in use. It is formed of a series of Rings connected with Chains, and when in use these are suspended from an Iron Standard. These Collapsible Trainers can be made any height or diameter, and Triangular, or any shape required.

SHOWING TRAINER COLLAPSED.

Further information, prices, etc. can be obtained from the Patentees and Manufacturers:—

SMITH, FLETCHER & CO.,
Wirework Manufacturers,
172, High Street, EDINBURGH.

TELEGRAMS—"NETTING," EDINBURGH.   TELEPHONE—No. 791.

Garden Wirework of Every Description.

SUTTON'S

SWEET PEAS.

SUTTON'S COLOUR SCHEMES.

Although a general mixture of Sweet Peas is very ornamental for the garden, there are cases where a more definite colour scheme is desired, and the following very pretty combinations will serve as a basis for those who may be planning such harmonies or contrasts.

Pink, Yellow and Salmon shades,
White and Pale Blue shades,
Pale Blue and Cream shades,
Salmon Pink and Pale Blue shades,
Rose Pink and Pale Blue shades,
Cream and Maroon shades,
Salmon Pink and Crimson shades,
Imperial Red, White and Blue,

Each, per packet, 2/6 and 1/-.

SUTTON'S COLLECTIONS of the NEWEST AND FINEST VARIETIES.

	£	s.	d
100 Sorts, our selection	2	10	0
50 ,, ,, ,,	1	7	6
25 ,, ,, ,,		15	0
18 ,, ,, ,,		10	6

Illustrated Catalogue of all the Best Varieties Post Free.

SUTTON'S GIANT FLOWERED.

In separate colours and in mixture.
Per packet, 1/-.

SUTTON & SONS, the King's Seedsmen, READING.

SWEET PEAS

IF YOU WANT

REALLY GOOD SWEET PEAS
AT MODERATE PRICES, SEND TO
ROBERT SYDENHAM LIMITED,
TENBY STREET, BIRMINGHAM,

No one will serve you better.

SPECIAL COLLECTIONS FOR 1910.

EACH PACKET in Nos. 1, 2 and 3 **CONTAINS 50 SELECTED SEEDS.**
Buyers not wanting any collection complete, may select their own varieties from EITHER COLLECTION at prices mentioned, and have 2/6 worth for each 2/-.

COLLECTION No. 1.—12 useful varieties, 1/3.

Dainty, Dorothy Eckford, Gladys Unwin, Henry Eckford, Hon. Mrs. Kenyon, Jeannie Gordon, Miss Willmott, Navy Blue, Queen of Spain, Romolo Piazzani, Saloplan, Triumph.

COLLECTION No. 2.—12 good varieties, 1/9.

A. J. Cook, Duke of Westminster, Evelyn Byatt, King Edward VII., Lady Grizel Hamilton, Lord Nelson, Lucy Hemus, Mrs. Collier, Nora Unwin, Paradise, Prince of Wales, Sybil Eckford.

Single Packets of any variety in Collections Nos. 1 and 2, 2d. each.

COLLECTIONS Nos. 1 and 2, when bought together, will be 2/6, and a packet each of **Janet Scott** and **Jet** will be added free of charge.

COLLECTION No. 3.—12 best varieties, 2/6.

Black Knight, Chrissie Unwin, Clara Curtis, Countess Spencer, Etta Dyke, Frank Dolby, George Herbert, Helen Lewis, Helen Pierce, Mrs. Hardcastle Sykes (30 *Seeds only as this variety partly failed*), Mrs. Walter Wright, Queen Alexandra.

Single Packets of any variety in Collection No. 3, 2d. each.

COLLECTIONS Nos. 2 and 3 may be had together for 3/6, and a packet each of **Phenomenal** and **Millie Maslin** will be added free of charge.

SPECIAL PRICE for the Three Collections, 4/6.

and when bought together the four added packets and a packet each of the four best striped varieties, viz.: **Jessie Cuthbertson, Mrs. J. Chamberlain, Prince Olaf** and **Unique** will be added free of charge, making 44 of the very best varieties in cultivation, at an average cost of about 1d. a packet.

COLLECTION No. 4.—The 12 newest varieties, 4/.-

Or what we consider the best of the newest.

SPECIAL NOTICE.—The price of, and number of Seeds of each variety in collection No. 4 varies. The number of seeds in each packet is stated in figures after each name. Any variety not priced cannot be sold apart from the collection.

Apple Blossom Spencer (40), rosy pink and blush, waved, 6d.; **America Spencer (15)**, bright rosy-scarlet flake, waved; **Black Knight Spencer (25)**, rich dark maroon, waved, 6d.; **Constance Oliver (20)**, creamy buff ground, flushed deep pink, waved; **Evelyn Hemus (20)**, waved, primrose with picotee edge of pink, 6d.; **Marjorie Willis (15)**, a Prince of Wales Spencer; **Miriam Beaver (6)**, a pinkish salmon on buff ground, 6d.; **Mrs. Charles Foster** or **Asta Ohn (20)**, beautiful waved lavenders, 9d.; **Paradise Ivory (20)**, a pale primrose with slight tinge of pink, waved, 8d.; **St. George (40)**, a grand orange scarlet, 6d.; **Sunproof Crimson Spencer (6)**, a large, well waved, rich crimson, a much improved The King, and absolutely sunproof, 1/-; **The Marquis (15)**, a large waved rosy mauve.

COLLECTIONS Nos. 3 and 4 may be had together for 5/6, and a packet of the New White Everlasting Pea, **White Pearl**, 25 Seeds, added free of charge.

SPECIAL PRICE for the Four Collections, 7/6.

OLD FAVOURITES OF MY RAISING.
Gladys Unwin.
Frank Dolby.
A. J. Cook.
Nora Unwin.
E. J. Castle.

W. J. UNWIN,
Histon,
CAMBRIDGE.

To enjoy Sweet Peas fully the grower must have Pure Stocks of The Best Varieties.

Beautiful Old and New Sweet Peas.

Unwin's Sweet Peas have won a High Reputation for Well-selected Stocks and Reliable Novelties.

Descriptive Price List post free.

W. J. UNWIN,
Histon,
CAMBRIDGE.

SOME OF MY LATEST CHAMPIONS.
Mrs. W. J. Unwin.
Douglas Unwin.
Gladys Burt.
Edna Unwin.